Canadian Living's Best

Cookies and Squares

BY
Elizabeth Baird
AND
The Food Writers of Canadian Living® Magazine
and The Canadian Living Test Kitchen

A MADISON PRESS BOOK
PRODUCED FOR
BALLANTINE BOOKS AND CANADIAN LIVING

Ballantine Books	Canadian Living
A Division of	Telemedia
Random House of	Communications Inc.
Canada Limited	25 Sheppard Avenue West
2775 Matheson Blvd East	Suite 100
Mississauga, Ontario	North York, Ontario
Canada	Canada
L4W 4P7	M2N 6S7

Canadian Cataloguing in Publication Data

Baird, Elizabeth
Cookies and Squares

(Canadian Living's best)
"Produced for Ballantine Books and Canadian Living."
Includes index.
ISBN 0-345-39870-X

1. Cookies. 2. Squares (Cookery). I. Title. II. Series.
TX772.B354 1998   641.8'654   C98-931335-2

EDITORIAL DIRECTOR: Hugh Brewster
PROJECT EDITOR: Wanda Nowakowska
EDITORIAL ASSISTANCE: Beverley Renahan, Rosemary Hillary
PRODUCTION DIRECTOR: Susan Barrable
PRODUCTION COORDINATOR: Donna Chong
BOOK DESIGN AND LAYOUT: Gordon Sibley Design Inc.
COLOR SEPARATION: Colour Technologies
PRINTING AND BINDING: Imprimeries Transcontinental Inc.

CANADIAN LIVING ADVISORY BOARD: Elizabeth Baird, Bonnie Baker Cowan,
Anna Hobbs, Caren King

CANADIAN LIVING'S BEST COOKIES AND SQUARES
was produced by Madison Press Books
which is under the direction of Albert E. Cummings

Madison Press Books
40 Madison Avenue
Toronto, Ontario, Canada
M5R 2S1

Printed in Canada

Contents

Lace Cookies (p. 16)

Caramel Pecan Brownies (p. 78)

Jam-Filled Sugar Cookies (p. 38)

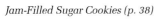

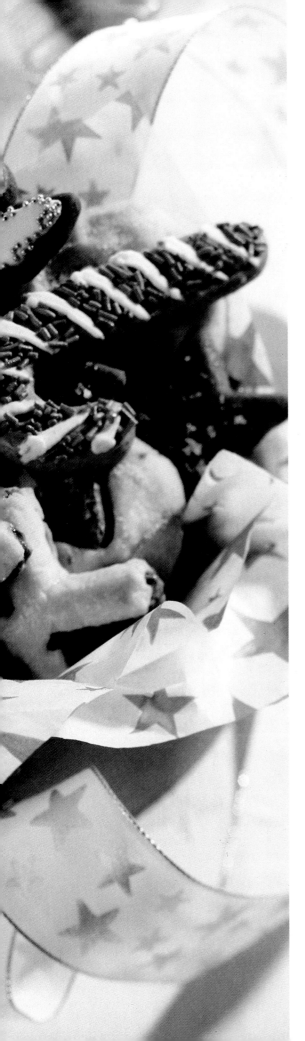

Introduction

W hat's so great about cookies?

Let me tell you why we love them so much at *Canadian Living*. First, they're so easy to make — especially drop cookies, or any kind of bar or square. Even fledgling cooks can be proud of their efforts. Then, ever culinarily curious, we never get tired of the many flavors these morsels come in — dimpled with chocolate, aromatic with cinnamon and ginger, or tangy with lemon or cranberries.

But flavor is just part of the pleasure that cookies bring. There's also the multitude of textures just waiting to be enjoyed in a single bite. Crisp and crunchy, or chewy with oats and coconut, cake-like and fudgy — or melt-in-your-mouth creamy like only shortbread can be. Who can resist?

Then there's the simple emotional appeal of cookies. Think back to weekend afternoons spent in the kitchen with your mother or grandmother baking family-favorite cookies. What better way to pass on recipes and skills — or to bond with your own children. And cookies invite sharing. If the batch makes three dozen, there's more than enough to pass on to family and friends.

Let *Canadian Living's Best Cookies and Squares* rekindle the pleasure of making — and sharing — new and favorite cookies. We guarantee you'll enjoy this delicious assortment, right down to the last crumb!

Elizabeth Baird

On front cover: Jam-Filled Sugar Cookies (p. 38) in the shape of stars, Megamocha Brownies (p. 82), Pistachio Shortbread (p. 56)

Drop-and-Bake Cookies

Drop cookies are as easy as one, two, three — just mix, drop onto baking sheets and bake. There's no faster way to fill up a cookie jar or to have cookies on hand for snacks and elegant dessert endings.

Chocolate Chip Ice Cream Sandies ▶

Canadian Living's 1998 Great Home-Cooking Mom Contest winner in Saskatoon, Holly Mitzel, makes these scrumptious chocolate chip cookies to sandwich around ice cream. Pure party fare!

Per sandwich (including ice cream): about
- 915 calories
- 9 g protein
- 54 g fat
- 109 g carbohydrate
- high source of fiber
- excellent source of iron

1 cup	butter, softened	250 mL
1-1/4 cups	packed brown sugar	300 mL
1	egg	1
1 tsp	vanilla	5 mL
2 cups	all-purpose flour	500 mL
1 tsp	baking soda	5 mL
1/4 tsp	salt	1 mL
2 cups	chocolate chips	500 mL
1 cup	raisins or chopped toasted pecans (optional)	250 mL
4 cups	vanilla ice cream	1 L
1 cup	mini colored chocolate chips	250 mL

● In large bowl, beat butter with sugar until light and fluffy; beat in egg and vanilla. In separate bowl, stir together flour, baking soda and salt; stir into butter mixture just until combined. Stir in chocolate chips, and raisins (if using).

● Drop by 1/4 cups (50 mL), about 2 inches (5 cm) apart, onto ungreased baking sheets. Bake in 350°F (180°C) oven for 15 minutes or until light brown. Let cool on pans for 3 minutes. Transfer to racks; let cool completely.

● Meanwhile, let ice cream soften in refrigerator for 20 minutes. Spread half of the cookies with 1/2 cup (125 mL) each of the ice cream. Top with remaining cookies, pressing gently to spread ice cream to edge. Roll edges in coloured chocolate chips.

● Wrap individually in plastic wrap and freeze for at least 4 hours or until firm. Makes 8 cookie sandwiches.

Double Chocolate Chunk Cookies ▼

Chock-full of big chunks of dark and white chocolate, these chewy cookies are sure to please any chocoholic or cookie lover. And we guarantee they'll go quickly at bake sales and cookie bazaars.

Per cookie: about
- 120 calories
- 1 g protein
- 6 g fat
- 15 g carbohydrate

1 cup	butter, softened	250 mL
1 cup	packed brown sugar	250 mL
1/2 cup	granulated sugar	125 mL
2	eggs	2
2 tsp	vanilla	10 mL
2-3/4 cups	all-purpose flour	675 mL
1 tsp	baking soda	5 mL
1/2 tsp	salt	2 mL
5 oz	each semisweet and white chocolate, coarsely chopped	150 g

● In large bowl, beat butter until fluffy; beat in brown and granulated sugars until smooth. Beat in eggs, one at a time; beat in vanilla.

● In separate bowl, stir together flour, baking soda and salt; stir into butter mixture in three additions. Stir in semisweet and white chocolate.

● Drop by rounded tablespoonfuls (15 mL), about 2-1/2 inches (6 cm) apart, onto greased baking sheets; flatten slightly.

● Bake in 350°F (180°C) oven for about 10 minutes, 12 minutes for frozen, or until edges are golden and centers still soft. Makes about 48 cookies.

TIPS

● You can freeze the portioned-out spoonfuls of dough on a baking sheet; when hard, bag and return them to the freezer for up to 1 month. Bake as many as you need at a time.

● You can substitute 1 bag (300 g) semisweet chocolate chips or 1 cup (250 mL) each white and dark chocolate chips for semisweet and white chocolate.

● For higher, more rounded cookies, cover and refrigerate on baking sheets for 30 minutes before baking; increase baking time by about 2 minutes.

STORING CHOCOLATE

● Wrap, then overwrap, chocolate to prevent moisture and odor absorption. Store in cool, dry place for up to six months.

● If you've had chocolate on hand for a while and it has developed a grey or white film, don't be alarmed. This slight discoloration, called "bloom,"

results from exposure to moisture or extreme changes in temperature. Once chocolate is melted, the discoloration will disappear.

● Frozen chocolate should always be thawed completely without unwrapping in order to prevent moisture from developing on the surface.

Jumbo Chipper

1/2 cup	butter, softened	125 mL
1/2 cup	shortening	125 mL
2/3 cup	packed brown sugar	150 mL
1/2 cup	granulated sugar	125 mL
2	eggs	2
1 tsp	vanilla	5 mL
1-1/2 cups	all-purpose flour	375 mL
1-1/2 cups	quick-cooking rolled oats	375 mL
1/2 tsp	baking soda	2 mL
1/2 tsp	each cinnamon and ground nutmeg	2 mL
1 cup	raisins	250 mL
1 cup	chocolate chips	250 mL
2/3 cup	chopped pecans (optional)	150 mL

● In large bowl, beat together butter, shortening, brown sugar and granulated sugar until creamy; beat in eggs and vanilla. In separate bowl, stir together flour, rolled oats, baking soda, cinnamon and nutmeg; stir into butter mixture. Stir in raisins, chocolate chips, and pecans (if using).

● Divide dough in half; place each on ungreased 12-inch (30 cm) round pizza pan. Place waxed paper over dough; press to spread dough evenly to edge of pan. Peel off paper. Bake in 350°F (180°C) oven for 15 to 20 minutes or until golden. Let cool on pan on rack for 10 minutes.

● Invert baking sheet onto cookie. Flip over and lift off pizza pan. Invert onto rack; let cool. Makes two 12-inch (30 cm) cookies, 8 servings each.

*P*at chocolate chip-filled dough onto a pizza pan for a giant of a cookie. For birthdays and other special occasions, add your own message in icing and package the cookie in a pizza-size box.

Per serving: about
- 335 calories
- 4 g protein
- 17 g fat
- 44 g carbohydrate

TIPS

● Use a pastry bag and plain tip to write the message in icing or melted chocolate.

● To transport cookie without breakage, layer between waxed paper on a clean pan, then wrap the whole thing in foil. (If you wish, place an inverted pan on top and tape the pans together.)

Black Forest Cookies

1-1/2 cups	semisweet chocolate chips	375 mL
1/2 cup	butter, softened	125 mL
1/2 cup	shortening	125 mL
1 cup	granulated sugar	250 mL
2	eggs	2
2 tsp	vanilla	10 mL
2 cups	all-purpose flour	500 mL
1/2 cup	unsweetened cocoa powder	125 mL
1 tsp	baking powder	5 mL
1/2 tsp	salt	2 mL
1 cup	dried cherries	250 mL

● In small bowl over saucepan of hot (not boiling) water, melt 1/2 cup (125 mL) of the chocolate chips; let cool.

● In large bowl, beat together butter, shortening and sugar until fluffy; beat in eggs, one at a time. Beat in vanilla, then melted chocolate. In separate bowl, stir together flour, cocoa, baking powder and salt; stir into butter mixture. Stir in cherries and remaining chocolate chips.

● Drop by tablespoonfuls (15 mL), about 2 inches (5 cm) apart, onto greased baking sheets. Bake in 375°F (190°C) oven for about 12 minutes or until edges are firm and centers still soft. Makes 42 cookies.

*T*art dried cherries in a rich, dark and moist chocolate cookie make these tasty mouthfuls special-occasion fare. For an attractive finish, drizzle melted bittersweet chocolate over the cooled cookies.

Per cookie: about
- 131 calories
- 2 g protein
- 7 g fat
- 16 g carbohydrate

Oatmeal Cookies (clockwise from top right): Fruit and Spice, Oatmeal Toffee Crunch, Oatmeal Raisin (two) and Lemon Coconut

Chocolate Chip Pumpkin Hermits

*H*ere's a dream cookie for lovers of pumpkin pie and chocolate.

Per cookie: about
- 92 calories
- 4 g fat
- 1 g protein
- 13 g carbohydrate

3/4 cup	shortening	175 mL
1-1/4 cups	packed brown sugar	300 mL
2	eggs	2
1 cup	pumpkin purée	250 mL
1 tsp	vanilla	5 mL
2 cups	all-purpose flour	500 mL
1 tsp	each baking powder and cinnamon	5 mL
1/2 tsp	each baking soda and salt	2 mL
1/2 tsp	each ground nutmeg, allspice and cloves	2 mL
1 cup	each raisins and chocolate chips	250 mL
1/2 cup	each chopped dates and nuts	125 mL

● In large bowl, beat shortening with sugar; beat in eggs, pumpkin and vanilla. In separate bowl, stir together flour, baking powder, cinnamon, baking soda, salt, nutmeg, allspice and cloves; stir into sugar mixture. Stir in raisins, chocolate chips, dates and nuts.

● Drop by rounded teaspoonfuls (5 mL), about 2 inches (5 cm) apart, onto greased baking sheets. Bake in 350°F (180°C) oven for 10 to 12 minutes or until golden brown. Makes about 60 cookies.

Oatmeal Cookies Five Ways ◄

1/2 cup	butter, softened	125 mL
3-1/4 cups	Best Oatmeal Cookie Mix (recipe follows)	800 mL
1	egg, beaten	1
4 tsp	water	20 mL
1 tsp	vanilla	5 mL

● In large bowl, beat butter into Best Cookie Mix at low speed until blended. Stir in egg, water and vanilla.

● Drop by tablespoonfuls (15 mL), about 2 inches (5 cm) apart, onto greased baking sheets. Bake in 375°F (190°C) oven for about 10 minutes or until golden. Makes about 36 cookies.

VARIATIONS

● OATMEAL TOFFEE CRUNCH COOKIES: Add 1 cup (250 mL) chopped milk chocolate-covered toffee bar, chocolate chips or peanut butter chips after beating butter into Mix.

● OATMEAL RAISIN COOKIES: Add 1 cup (250 mL) raisins and 1 tsp (5 mL) cinnamon after beating butter into Mix. Bake for 12 minutes.

● FRUIT AND SPICE COOKIES: Omit vanilla. Add 1/2 cup (125 mL) each chopped candied fruit, walnuts and raisins, 1 tsp (5 mL) cinnamon, 1/2 tsp (2 mL) nutmeg and 1/4 tsp (1 mL) ground cloves after beating butter into Mix.

● LEMON COCONUT COOKIES: Omit vanilla. Add 1/2 cup (125 mL) shredded coconut and 2 tsp (10 mL) grated lemon rind after beating butter into Mix.

BEST OATMEAL COOKIE MIX		
4-1/2 cups	all-purpose flour	1.125 L
4-1/2 cups	quick-cooking rolled oats	1.125 L
4 cups	packed brown sugar	1 L
1 tbsp	baking soda	15 mL
1 tbsp	baking powder	15 mL
2 tsp	salt	10 mL

● In large bowl, stir together flour, rolled oats, sugar, baking soda, baking powder and salt. Transfer to airtight container; store in cool, dry place for up to 2 months. Stir well before using. Makes 13 cups (3.25 L).

When you have a cookie that's popular with everyone, why not stir up a convenient master mix that anyone in the house can use. Here's that cookie lovers' mix plus four fabulous variations.

Per cookie: about
• 72 calories   • 1 g protein
• 3 g fat   • 11 g carbohydrate

TIP: Refrigerating the spoonfuls of dough on baking sheets for 15 minutes before baking yields thicker, chewier cookies.

Oatmeal Chocolate Chip Crispies

1 cup	butter, softened	250 mL
3/4 cup	packed brown sugar	175 mL
1/2 cup	granulated sugar	125 mL
2	eggs	2
1-1/2 tsp	vanilla	7 mL
2 cups	all-purpose flour	500 mL
1 cup	rice crisp cereal	250 mL
1 cup	quick-cooking rolled oats	250 mL
1 tsp	baking soda	5 mL
Pinch	salt	Pinch
1-1/2 cups	chocolate chips	375 mL

● In large bowl, beat butter with brown and granulated sugars until light and fluffy. Beat in eggs, one at a time; beat in vanilla. In separate bowl, stir together flour, cereal, rolled oats, baking soda and salt; stir into butter mixture. Stir in chocolate chips.

● Drop by heaping tablespoonfuls (15 mL), about 2 inches (5 cm) apart, onto greased baking sheets. Bake in 350°F (180°C) oven for 10 to 12 minutes or until edges are crisp and golden. Makes about 60 cookies.

Crispy rice cereal adds new crackle and pop to the ever-popular oatmeal and chocolate chip combo.

Per cookie: about
• 90 calories   • 1 g protein
• 5 g fat   • 11 g carbohydrate

NUT KNOW-HOW

● To ensure freshness, buy nuts from a store with a high turnover. Bulk stores often have the freshest nuts; if possible, sample nuts before buying.

● Most nuts taste better in cookies if they're toasted. Spread nuts in single layer on baking sheet; toast in the oven (or toaster oven, for small amounts) at 350°F (180°C) for 8 to 10 minutes or until darkened slightly, stirring once or twice if quantities are large. Watch carefully because nuts brown quickly once they're hot.

● To toast nuts in the microwave, spread nuts on microwaveable plate; microwave at High for 5 to 10 minutes or until fragrant, stirring every 2 minutes.

● To remove skins from hazelnuts, rub hot toasted hazelnuts in a clean terry towel until most or all of the skins are removed. Some people like the color and taste that the toasted skin adds to cookies: if so, rub the hazelnuts lightly to retain some of the brown skins.

● Store nuts in the freezer to ensure freshness.

Hermits Galore

W*e don't know how these spicy drops — here with six fabulous variations — came to be known as hermits. Maybe because, once the word got out about how good they were, you had to lock yourself away with the cookies like a hermit or everybody else would help themselves. Just kidding!*

Per cookie: about
- 77 calories
- 4 g fat
- 1 g protein
- 11 g carbohydrate

1/2 cup	butter, softened	125 mL
1/2 cup	shortening	125 mL
1 cup	packed brown sugar	250 mL
1/3 cup	granulated sugar	75 mL
2	eggs	2
1 tsp	vanilla	5 mL
2-1/2 cups	all-purpose flour	625 mL
1 tsp	each baking powder and cinnamon	5 mL
3/4 tsp	each ground nutmeg, allspice and cloves	4 mL
1/2 tsp	each baking soda and salt	2 mL
1-1/2 cups	raisins	375 mL
1 cup	chopped dates	250 mL
1 cup	chopped toasted pecans	250 mL

● In large bowl, beat together butter, shortening, brown sugar and granulated sugar until light and fluffy. Beat in eggs, one at a time; beat in vanilla.

● In separate bowl, stir together flour, baking powder, cinnamon, nutmeg, allspice, cloves, baking soda and salt; stir into butter mixture. Stir in raisins, dates and pecans.

● Drop by tablespoonfuls (15 mL), about 2 inches (5 cm) apart, onto greased baking sheets. Bake in 350°F (180°C) oven for about 15 minutes or until golden. Makes about 80 cookies.

VARIATIONS

● MOUNTAIN MAN: Omit raisins, dates and pecans. Substitute 3-1/2 cups (875 mL) trail mix.

● ROBINSON CRUSOE: Omit raisins, dates and pecans. Substitute 1/2 cup (125 mL) chopped dried papaya, 3/4 cup (175 mL) chopped dried pineapple, 1-1/4 cups (300 mL) coconut and 1 cup (250 mL) chopped toasted macadamia or Brazil nuts.

● MORNING GRUMP: Omit dates and pecans. Substitute 1-1/4 cups (300 mL) rice crisp cereal and 3/4 cup (175 mL) roasted peanuts.

● GRETA GARBOS: Substitute 1/2 tsp (2 mL) cardamom for the ground cloves. Omit raisins, dates and pecans. Substitute 2 cups (500 mL) candied fruit, 1-1/2 cups (375 mL) chopped toasted almonds and 2 tsp (10 mL) each grated orange rind and lemon rind.

● HEIDI'S HERMITS: Omit raisins, dates and pecans. Substitute 3 cups (750 mL) chopped nougat milk chocolate bars or chocolate chips.

● BIRTHDAY HERMITS: Omit raisins, dates and pecans. Substitute 2 cups (500 mL) baking gums or candy-coated chocolate candies.

Cardamom Orange Cookies

3/4 cup	butter, softened	175 mL
3/4 cup	granulated sugar	175 mL
1	egg	1
1 tbsp	grated orange rind	15 mL
1 tsp	vanilla	5 mL
1-1/2 cups	all-purpose flour	375 mL
1/2 cup	ground almonds	125 mL
1-1/4 tsp	ground cardamom	6 mL
1 tsp	baking powder	5 mL
Pinch	salt	Pinch

● In large bowl, beat butter with sugar until light and fluffy; beat in egg, orange rind and vanilla. In separate bowl, stir together flour, almonds, cardamom, baking powder and salt; stir into butter mixture.

● Drop by tablespoonfuls (15 mL), about 2 inches (5 cm) apart, onto greased baking sheets. Bake in 350°F (180°C) oven for about 10 minutes or until edges are golden. Makes 36 cookies.

Cardamom, a pleasing spice usually associated with curries and Indian cooking, is also traditional in Scandinavian baking. It pairs delightfully with zesty orange rind in these cookies with crispy edges and tender cake-like centers.

Per cookie: about
- 80 calories
- 1 g protein
- 5 g fat
- 9 g carbohydrate

Caribbean Drops

2/3 cup	butter, softened	150 mL
1 cup	granulated sugar	250 mL
1/4 cup	fancy molasses	50 mL
2 tbsp	dark rum	25 mL
1	egg	1
2 cups	all-purpose flour	500 mL
1 tsp	each baking soda and cinnamon	5 mL
3/4 tsp	ground allspice	4 mL
1/2 tsp	ground ginger	2 mL
1-1/4 cups	shredded coconut	300 mL
	TOPPING	
1 tbsp	granulated sugar	15 mL

● In large bowl, beat butter with sugar until light and fluffy; beat in molasses and rum. Beat in egg. In separate bowl, stir together flour, baking soda, cinnamon, allspice and ginger; stir into butter mixture. Stir in coconut.

● Drop by tablespoonfuls (15 mL), about 2 inches (5 cm) apart, onto greased baking sheets.

● TOPPING: Sprinkle cookies with sugar. Bake in 350°F (180°C) oven for about 12 minutes or until browned, edges are set and centers still slightly soft. Makes about 54 cookies.

With a touch of spice, Caribbean molasses and shredded coconut, these easy-to-make drops are a wonderful teatime treat. Or serve with sherbets in a rainbow of fruit flavors such as mango, raspberry and lemon.

Per cookie: about
- 69 calories
- 1 g protein
- 3 g fat
- 10 g carbohydrate

TIP: For shaped cookies, increase sugar topping to 1/2 cup (125 mL); roll dough into 1-inch (2.5 cm) balls and roll in sugar.

SOFT OR CRISP COOKIES?

● Refrigerating spoonfuls of raw dough on baking sheets until firm, about 15 minutes, yields thicker, chewier cookies.

● Baking drop cookies immediately yields a flatter, crisper cookie.

Thumbprint Cookies ◄

3/4 cup	butter, softened	175 mL
1/2 cup	packed brown sugar	125 mL
1/4 cup	granulated sugar	50 mL
2	eggs	2
1 tsp	vanilla	5 mL
1-3/4 cups	all-purpose flour	425 mL
1 tsp	baking soda	5 mL
1/2 tsp	salt	2 mL
1-1/2 cups	mini chocolate chips	375 mL
	FILLING	
3/4 cup	smooth peanut butter	175 mL
1/3 cup	icing sugar	75 mL
2 tbsp	butter, softened	25 mL
	GARNISH	
1/3 cup	chocolate sprinkles or mini chocolate chips	75 mL

● In large bowl, beat together butter, brown sugar and granulated sugar until light. Beat in eggs, one at a time; beat in vanilla. In separate bowl, stir together flour, baking soda and salt; stir into butter mixture. Stir in chocolate chips. Let stand for 10 minutes.

● Drop by tablespoonfuls (15 mL) into 1-inch (2.5 cm) mounds, about 2 inches (5 cm) apart, onto greased baking sheets. Bake in 350°F (180°C) oven for 10 to 12 minutes or until golden. Using melon baller or small spoon, press indentation into each cookie. *(Cookies can be prepared to this point, frozen on baking sheet, then stored in layers between waxed paper in rigid airtight container for up to 3 weeks; thaw to continue.)*

● FILLING: In bowl, beat together peanut butter, icing sugar and butter until smooth; spoon rounded teaspoonful (5 mL) into hollow of each cookie.

● GARNISH: Sprinkle cookies with chocolate sprinkles. Makes about 48 cookies.

Combine two flavor favorites — chocolate and peanut butter — in a cookie kids will be happy to help you make.

Per cookie: about
- 122 calories
- 8 g fat
- 2 g protein
- 12 g carbohydrate

Cherry Vanilla Jumbles

1/2 cup	butter, softened	125 mL
3/4 cup	granulated sugar	175 mL
1	egg	1
2 tsp	vanilla	10 mL
1/4 cup	sour cream	50 mL
1-3/4 cups	all-purpose flour	425 mL
1/2 tsp	baking powder	2 mL
Pinch	salt	Pinch
3/4 cup	dried sour cherries	175 mL
2 tbsp	icing sugar	25 mL

● In large bowl, beat butter with sugar until light and fluffy; beat in egg and vanilla. Beat in sour cream. In separate bowl, stir together flour, baking powder and salt; stir into butter mixture. Stir in dried cherries. Cover with plastic wrap and refrigerate for 30 minutes. *(Dough can be refrigerated for up to 2 days.)*

● Drop by tablespoonfuls (15 mL), about 2 inches (5 cm) apart, onto greased baking sheets. Bake in 350°F (180°C) oven for about 12 minutes or until tops are set and bottoms are golden. Let cool on pan on rack for 5 minutes; transfer to rack and let cool completely. Dust with icing sugar. Makes 36 cookies.

Dried cherries are a delight in these soft cookies but you can substitute dried blueberries, cranberries, snipped apricots or (for true pleasure seekers) chocolate chips.

Per cookie: about
- 75 calories
- 3 g fat
- 1 g protein
- 11 g carbohydrate

Thumbprint Cookies (bottom) and Oatmeal Butterscotch Triangles (p. 57)

Lace Cookies ▶

Temperature is all-important when it comes to these crisp candy-like cookies. You can let them cool flat and lacy — or shape them around a thick wooden spoon handle or broomstick while they're still quite hot and you have brandy snaps.

Per cookie: about
- 31 calories
- 1 g fat
- trace protein
- 5 g carbohydrate

1/4 cup	packed brown sugar	50 mL
1/4 cup	butter	50 mL
1/4 cup	corn syrup	50 mL
1/3 cup	all-purpose flour	75 mL
1/2 tsp	vanilla	2 mL

● In saucepan, bring sugar, butter and corn syrup to boil over medium heat. Remove from heat; whisk in flour, 1 tbsp (15 mL) water and vanilla until smooth.

● Making six cookies at a time, drop scant teaspoonfuls (5 mL) batter for each cookie, about 3 inches (8 cm) apart, onto large parchment paper-lined baking sheet. Bake in 350°F (180°C) oven for 5 to 6 minutes or until golden.

● Let stand on pan on rack for 1 minute or until slightly set but still soft enough to roll, if desired. Transfer to rack; let cool completely. Makes 30 cookies.

VARIATION
● ALMOND CARDAMOM LACE COOKIES: Add 1/4 cup (50 mL) sliced almonds and 3/4 tsp (4 mL) ground cardamom along with flour.

TO MAKE LACE TRIANGLES
● To make tall triangles as in photo, use 2 tbsp (25 mL) batter for each cookie and drop, two at a time and about 6 inches (15 cm) apart, onto baking sheet. Bake for 10 to 12 minutes or until golden. Let stand on pan on rack for 1 minute or until slightly set but still soft enough to cut.
● With pizza wheel or small sharp knife, cut each cookie in half. Cut each half into 1 long triangle, reserving leftover pieces of cookie. Transfer to smooth dry surface; let cool completely. Makes 8 triangles.

TIP: Serve triangles with dessert. Crumble leftover cookies to sprinkle over or into softened ice cream.

Chocolate Pecan Kisses

A piping bag speeds up forming these feather-light treats but a small spoon works well, too.

Per cookie: about
- 25 calories
- 1 g fat
- 1 g protein
- 4 g carbohydrate

3	egg whites	3
1/4 tsp	cream of tartar	1 mL
3/4 cup	granulated sugar	175 mL
1/2 cup	finely chopped pecans or walnuts	125 mL
1/4 cup	sifted unsweetened cocoa powder	50 mL
1/2 tsp	vanilla	2 mL
Pinch	salt	Pinch

● In large bowl, beat egg whites with cream of tartar until soft peaks form; beat in sugar, 2 tbsp (25 mL) at a time, until stiff glossy peaks form. Fold in pecans, cocoa powder, vanilla and salt.

● Spoon into pastry bag fitted with 1/2-inch (1 cm) tip; pipe 1-inch (2.5 cm) kisses, about 1-1/2 inches (4 cm) apart, onto greased baking sheets. Bake in 250°F (120°C) oven for about 45 minutes or until outside is firm but inside slightly soft. Makes about 44 cookies.

Tulip Petal Cups ▲

For a spectacular finish to any special-occasion dinner, serve these elegant dessert cups filled with ice cream or fruit.

Per tulip petal cup: about
- 131 calories
- 2 g protein
- 5 g fat
- 19 g carbohydrate

1/3 cup	butter, softened	75 mL
2/3 cup	granulated sugar	150 mL
1 cup	all-purpose flour	250 mL
3	egg whites, lightly beaten	3
1 tsp	almond extract	5 mL

● In bowl, beat butter with sugar at medium speed for 2 minutes or until fluffy. Using wooden spoon, stir in flour, in two additions, until mixture is crumbly. Stir in egg whites, 1 tbsp (15 mL) at a time, until creamy. Stir in almond extract.

● Drop 2 tbsp (25 mL) onto half of well-greased baking sheet; spread with spatula or back of spoon to form 5-1/2-inch (13 cm) circle. Repeat on other half of sheet. Bake in 400°F (200°C) oven for 6 to 8 minutes or just until golden brown at edges.

● Working quickly, immediately slide palette knife under cookies and transfer each to 4-1/4-inch (11 cm) diameter bowls. Gently press into bowl with 2-1/2-inch (6 cm) diameter glass to form tulip shape. Repeat with remaining batter, using cool baking sheet. Makes 12 tulip petal cups.

TIP: When making the cookie cups, work quickly to avoid cooling, which can cause the cookies to crack.

Coconut Ginger Macaroons

2-3/4 cups	flaked coconut (200 g pkg)	675 mL
2/3 cup	granulated sugar	150 mL
1/3 cup	all-purpose flour	75 mL
1/4 tsp	salt	1 mL
4	egg whites	4
1/4 cup	finely chopped crystallized ginger	50 mL
1 tsp	vanilla	5 mL

● In large bowl, stir together coconut, sugar, flour and salt. Whisk egg whites until foamy; stir into coconut mixture along with ginger and vanilla.

● Drop by tablespoonfuls (15 mL), about 2 inches (5 cm) apart, onto greased baking sheets. Bake in 325°F (160°C) oven for 20 to 25 minutes or until edges are golden brown. Transfer immediately to rack to let cool. Makes about 36 cookies.

Ginger lovers are as dedicated to their flavor as chocolate lovers are to theirs. These easy-to-make sweeties, which are crisp on the outside and chewy on the inside, will satisfy even the most ardent ginger fan.

Per cookie: about
- 52 calories
- 2 g fat
- 1 g protein
- 9 g carbohydrate

Chocolate Wafers

1/2 cup	blanched almonds	125 mL
1/2 cup	hazelnuts	125 mL
1 cup	icing sugar	250 mL
1/4 cup	cornstarch	50 mL
3	egg whites	3
2 tbsp	butter, melted	25 mL
2 tbsp	hazelnut or almond liqueur	25 mL
6 oz	semisweet chocolate, coarsely chopped	175 g

● Spread almonds and hazelnuts on rimmed baking sheet. Bake in 350°F (180°C) oven for 8 to 10 minutes or until fragrant and browned. Transfer to tea towel; rub skins off hazelnuts.

● In food processor, combine almonds, hazelnuts, 1/3 cup (75 mL) of the sugar and cornstarch; chop coarsely. Transfer to bowl; set aside.

● In large bowl, beat egg whites until soft peaks form; beat in remaining sugar, 2 tbsp (25 mL) at a time, until stiff peaks form. Fold in nut mixture. Fold in butter and liqueur.

● Drop by tablespoonfuls (15 mL), about 2 inches (5 cm) apart, onto parchment paper-lined baking sheets. Bake in 325°F (160°C) oven for about 18 minutes or until browned and firm around edges but still soft in center. Transfer to racks; let cool.

● In bowl over saucepan of hot (not boiling) water, melt chocolate; spread about 1 tsp (5 mL) over bottom of each cookie. Using cake decorating comb or fork tines, make wavy lines in chocolate; let cool until set. Makes about 42 cookies.

Here's an elegant little hazelnut meringue cookie with chocolate spread over its bottom.

Per cookie: about
- 60 calories
- 4 g fat
- 1 g protein
- 6 g carbohydrate

TIP: If the chocolate gets too firm when you are assembling the cookies, set the bowl back over hot water to soften.

Chocolate Chow Mein Clusters

Hide these crispy no-bake treats — an addictive blend of chocolate, butterscotch, crunchy peanuts and dry chow mein noodles — unless, of course, you want them to disappear right away.

Per cluster: about
- 94 calories
- 7 g fat
- 2 g protein
- 7 g carbohydrate

1-1/2 cups	chocolate chips	375 mL
1 cup	butterscotch chips	250 mL
1/2 cup	butter	125 mL
1/4 cup	smooth peanut butter	50 mL
2 cups	dry chow mein noodles	500 mL
1 cup	salted peanuts	250 mL
50	candied cherry halves	50

● In bowl over saucepan of hot (not boiling) water, melt together chocolate and butterscotch chips, butter and peanut butter, stirring often.

● In large bowl, stir noodles with peanuts; pour in chocolate mixture and mix well.

● Spoon into 1-inch (2.5 cm) mounds on waxed paper-lined baking sheets; garnish each with cherry half. Let stand for 30 minutes or refrigerate for 20 minutes or until firm. Makes about 50 clusters.

Pignoli

These Italian macaroons, with a crisp outside and chewy heart, are named for their most important ingredient — pine nuts (pignoli).

Per cookie: about
- 56 calories
- 2 g fat
- 1 g protein
- 9 g carbohydrate

1	pkg (8 oz/220 g) marzipan	1
2	egg whites	2
1/2 cup	granulated sugar	125 mL
2 tsp	finely chopped lemon rind	10 mL
1/2 cup	toasted pine nuts	125 mL

● In food processor, coarsely chop marzipan; spread on baking sheet and let stand for 4 hours or until dry, or for up to 24 hours. Return to food processor; chop until fine crumbs form.

● In large bowl, beat egg whites until frothy; beat in sugar, 2 tbsp (25 mL) at a time, and lemon rind until soft peaks form. Fold in marzipan.

● Drop by tablespoonfuls (15 mL), about 2 inches (5 cm) apart, onto greased baking sheets. Top with pine nuts, lightly pressing with back of spoon. Bake in 350°F (180°C) oven for about 20 minutes or until evenly browned. Makes 32 cookies.

TIP: Slivered almonds can be used instead of pine nuts but the unique taste and texture that pine nuts bring to these cookies will definitely be missed.

TOP, CENTER OR BOTTOM RACK OF THE OVEN?

Positioning the baking sheet correctly in the oven ensures even baking and tasty results.

● Ideally, bake cookies, one baking sheet at a time, in the center of the oven. Check cookies near the end of the baking time to see that they are baking evenly. Rotate baking sheet, if necessary, to prevent cookies from over-baking in oven hot spot.

● In reality, most bakers need to speed up the baking process and opt for baking two sheets at a time. Set racks just below and just above center of oven; place baking sheets on rack. Rotate baking sheets and change racks halfway through time specified in recipe.

HOW TO MEASURE INGREDIENTS

Careful measuring of ingredients is important for best results when baking.

Measures

There are two types of measuring cups — one for dry ingredients and one for wet. Be sure to follow either metric or imperial measures all the way through the recipe, not a combination.

● Dry-ingredient measures come in sets of different sizes: 1/4 cup (50 mL); 1/3 cup (75 mL); 1/2 cup (125 mL); 1 cup (250 mL).

● Liquid-ingredient glass measuring cups have levels marked on the outside of them.

● Measuring spoons are used for small amounts of both dry and liquid ingredients: 1/4 tsp (1 mL); 1/2 tsp (2 mL); 1 tsp (5 mL); 1 tbsp (15 mL).

Dry Ingredients

● Lightly spoon the dry ingredient, such as flour or granulated sugar, into the dry measure.

● Do not pack it down or tap the measure on the counter. (The exception is brown sugar, which should be packed enough to keep its cup shape when dumped out.)

● Fill the measure until it is heaped up in a little mound. Then, working over the canister of flour or sugar, level off the mound by pushing the straight edge of a knife across the top of the measure.

Liquid Ingredients

● Place the liquid measure on the counter. Pour in the liquid to the desired level, then bend down to check the measurement at eye level.

● If the liquid doesn't come exactly to the desired mark on the outside, pour a little off or add a little, as needed.

Shape-and-Bake Cookies

Almost as fast as drop-and-bakes, the cookies in this stellar collection are either rolled into balls or shaped into logs and sliced before baking. These are great starter cookies for young bakers in the family.

Icebox Cookies Galore ▶

Cookie dough shaped into logs that are ready to slice and bake is an ideal way to enjoy cookies when you crave them — or need them in a hurry! Here's a basic rich butter-and-sugar dough with candied cherries, but you can be creative and try other add-ins (see Icebox Cookie Dress-Ups, p. 24).

Per cookie: about
- 50 calories
- 2 g fat
- 1 g protein
- 7 g carbohydrate

1 cup	butter, softened	250 mL
1 cup	granulated sugar	250 mL
1	egg	1
2 tsp	vanilla	10 mL
2-2/3 cups	all-purpose flour	650 mL
1/2 tsp	baking powder	2 mL
1/4 tsp	salt	1 mL
3/4 cup	chopped candied red or green cherries	175 mL

● In large bowl, beat butter with sugar until light and fluffy. Beat in egg and vanilla. In separate bowl, stir together flour, baking powder and salt; using wooden spoon, stir into butter mixture in two additions. Stir in candied cherries.

● Divide dough into thirds; scrape one third onto large piece of waxed paper. Using paper as guide, roll into 8-inch (20 cm) long log. Remove paper. Wrap in plastic wrap, twisting ends to seal.

● Repeat with remaining dough. Refrigerate for at least 3 hours or until firm. *(Logs can be refrigerated for up to 3 days or frozen for up to 3 weeks; thaw for 20 minutes.)*

● Cut into 1/4-inch (5 mm) thick slices; place, about 2 inches (5 cm) apart, on greased baking sheets. Bake in 375°F (190°C) oven for 10 to 12 minutes or until light brown. Makes about 84 cookies.

VARIATION

● DOUBLE-CHOCOLATE COOKIES: Reduce flour to 2-1/4 cups (550 mL). Add 1/2 cup (125 mL) unsweetened cocoa powder to flour mixture. Substitute 5 oz (150 g) white chocolate, finely chopped, for the candied cherries. Bake for 10 to 15 minutes.

FOR THE BEST COOKIES
● Make cookies the same size and shape for even browning.
● Always check cookies for doneness at the earliest time called for.

An assortment of Icebox Cookies: (from top right) coated in green sugar; topped with colored sprinkles; coated in white chocolate, then drizzled with melted bittersweet chocolate; chock-full of candied cherries. (For more decorating ideas, see p. 24.) In center: Double-Chocolate Cookies.

ICEBOX COOKIE DRESS-UPS

Here's how to dress up Icebox Cookies Galore (p. 22) to suit every taste and occasion.

Lots of Fun Add-Ins

For candied cherries, substitute any of the following: mini candies; mini chocolate or butterscotch chips; toffee pieces; candied ginger; chopped toasted pecans, almonds or walnuts.

Decadent Dress-Ups ▶

Omit candied cherries.
● Top still-warm baked cookies with colored or chocolate sprinkles.
● Or top baked and cooled cookies with melted white chocolate, then drizzle melted bittersweet chocolate back and forth on top.
● Or dip ends of cookies in melted chocolate and press chopped toasted nuts on top.

Coats of Many Colors

Omit candied cherries. Before refrigerating dough, roll it in candy sprinkles, coarse colored sugar or shredded coconut.

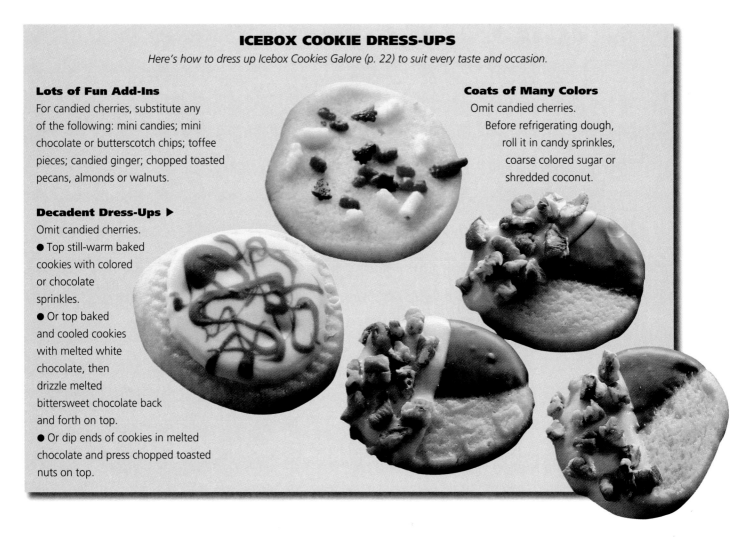

Glazed Poppy Seed Cookies

An egg glaze and sprinkle of poppy seeds brighten these light, buttery slices.

Per cookie: about
- 73 calories
- 5 g fat
- 1 g protein
- 7 g carbohydrate

1 cup	butter, softened	250 mL
3/4 cup	granulated sugar	175 mL
5	hard-cooked egg yolks	5
2 tsp	grated lemon rind	10 mL
1 tsp	vanilla	5 mL
1-3/4 cups	all-purpose flour	425 mL
1/4 tsp	salt	1 mL
1	egg	1
2 tbsp	poppy seeds	25 mL

● In large bowl, beat butter with sugar until light and fluffy; beat in egg yolks, lemon rind and vanilla until smooth. Stir in flour and salt just until dough forms.

● Divide dough in half; roll each into 2-inch (5 cm) diameter log. Wrap in plastic wrap and refrigerate for at least 1 hour or until chilled, or for up to 2 days.

● Cut into 1/4-inch (5 mm) thick slices; place, 2 inches (5 cm) apart, on greased baking sheets. Beat egg with 1 tsp (5 mL) water; brush over cookies. Sprinkle with poppy seeds.

● Bake in 350°F (180°C) oven for 12 to 15 minutes or until golden. Makes 48 cookies.

Peanut Butter Slice-and-Bakes ▼

2/3 cup	butter, softened	150 mL
2/3 cup	peanut butter	150 mL
1-1/3 cups	granulated sugar	325 mL
1	egg	1
1-1/2 tsp	vanilla	7 mL
2 cups	all-purpose flour	500 mL
3/4 tsp	baking soda	4 mL
1/4 tsp	salt	1 mL
2/3 cup	chopped peanuts	150 mL

● In large bowl, beat together butter, peanut butter and sugar until smooth; beat in egg and vanilla. In separate bowl, stir together flour, baking soda and salt; using wooden spoon, stir into butter mixture in two additions. Stir in peanuts.

● Divide dough into thirds; scrape one third onto large piece of waxed paper. Using paper as guide, roll into 8-inch (20 cm) long log. Remove paper. Wrap in plastic wrap, twisting ends to seal.

● Repeat with remaining dough. Refrigerate for at least 3 hours or until firm. *(Logs can be refrigerated for up to 3 days or frozen for up to 3 weeks; thaw for 20 minutes.)*

● Cut into 1/4-inch (5 mm) thick slices; place, about 2 inches (5 cm) apart, on greased baking sheets. Bake in 375°F (190°C) oven for 8 to 10 minutes or until light golden. Makes about 84 cookies.

VARIATION

● PEANUT BUTTER CHOCOLATE SWIRL SLICE-AND-BAKES: Increase all-purpose flour to 2-1/3 cups (575 mL). Omit chopped peanuts. In bowl over saucepan of hot (not boiling) water, melt 6 oz (175 g) bittersweet (not unsweetened) chocolate; set aside.

● Roll out each third of dough between waxed paper into 10- x 8-inch (25 x 20 cm) rectangle. Remove top paper. Spread each portion of dough with one-third of the chocolate. Using paper as guide, tightly roll up jelly roll-style. Remove paper. Wrap in plastic wrap, twisting ends to seal. *(Logs can be refrigerated for up to 3 days or frozen for up to 2 weeks; thaw for 20 minutes.)* Slice and bake for 10 to 15 minutes.

Τhis easy-to-handle dough swings two ways — no-fuss with chopped peanuts for quick treats, or rolled out and spread with chocolate, then rerolled for a pretty spiral effect. Both cookies are an attractive addition to a dainty tray, or pure pleasure in a gift package.

Per cookie: about
• 55 calories   • 1 g protein
• 3 g fat   • 6 g carbohydrate

Peanut Butter Chocolate Swirl Slice-and-Bakes (surrounded by an assortment of Icebox Cookies, p. 22)

Chocolate Hazelnut Slices

Either slice and bake these nutty cookies or shape them into crescents. Ground hazelnuts are available in many bulk food stores.

Per cookie: about
- 119 calories
- 9 g fat
- 1 g protein
- 10 g carbohydrate

1 cup	butter, softened	250 mL
1 cup	icing sugar	250 mL
1-1/2 cups	all-purpose flour	375 mL
1/2 cup	ground hazelnuts or almonds	125 mL
1/3 cup	unsweetened cocoa powder	75 mL
	GARNISH	
6 oz	semisweet chocolate, coarsely chopped	175 g
3/4 cup	ground hazelnuts	175 mL

● In large bowl, beat butter with sugar until fluffy. In separate bowl, stir together flour, nuts and cocoa; stir into butter mixture to form smooth dough.

● Gather dough into ball; divide in half. Place each half on sheet of waxed paper; using paper as guide, shape dough into logs, each about 1 inch (2.5 cm) in diameter. Wrap paper around logs and chill until firm.

● Cut into 1/4-inch (5 mm) thick slices; place, about 2 inches (5 cm) apart, on ungreased baking sheets. Bake in 325°F (160°C) oven for 15 minutes or until set. *(Cookies can be prepared to this point and frozen in rigid airtight container for up to 1 month; thaw before continuing.)*

● GARNISH: In bowl over saucepan of hot (not boiling) water, melt chocolate, stirring occasionally. Dip edges of cookies into chocolate, then into nuts. Let stand on rack until set. Makes about 60 cookies.

VARIATION
● CHOCOLATE HAZELNUT CRESCENTS: Chill dough in bowl for 30 minutes. Form by tablespoonfuls (15 mL) into crescents; chill on baking sheets for 30 minutes. Bake for about 30 minutes; dip ends in melted chocolate and sliced nuts. Makes about 36 cookies.

Danish Brune Kager ▶

Although the English translation is simply "brown cookies," it doesn't do these delicious gingerbready cookies justice. They're a must in every Danish household during Christmas and are especially pretty cut out in the traditional Scandinavian heart shape.

Per round cookie: about
- 52 calories
- 3 g fat
- 1 g protein
- 6 g carbohydrate

1 cup	butter, softened	250 mL
1 cup	granulated sugar	250 mL
1/2 cup	corn syrup	125 mL
2-3/4 cups	all-purpose flour	675 mL
1 cup	unblanched almonds, chopped	250 mL
1 tbsp	cinnamon	15 mL
2 tsp	each ginger and ground cloves	10 mL
1 tsp	baking soda	5 mL

● In large bowl, beat butter with sugar until creamy; stir in corn syrup. In separate bowl, stir together flour, almonds, cinnamon, ginger, cloves and baking soda; with wooden spoon, gradually stir into butter mixture to make soft, but not sticky, dough.

● Divide into quarters. On lightly floured surface, roll each into 1-1/2-inch (4 cm) diameter log. Wrap in plastic wrap and refrigerate until chilled. *(Dough can be refrigerated for 24 hours or frozen for up to 1 month; thaw before baking.)*

● Cut into 1/4-inch (5 mm) thick slices; place, 1 inch (2.5 cm) apart, on greased baking sheets. (Or roll out between waxed paper; cut, using 2-inch/5 cm heart-shaped cookie cutter.) Bake in 400°F (200°C) oven for 8 to 10 minutes or until golden brown. Makes about 96 round cookies or 72 heart-shaped cookies.

TIP: You can also roll out this dough just as you do gingerbread cookie dough (see p. 42).

(Clockwise from top) Finsk Brød, King's Bread (a fruit- and nut-filled log of marzipan coated with chocolate), Vanilla Wreaths (p. 53) and Danish Brune Kager (p. 26)

Finsk Brød ▲

2-1/3 cups	all-purpose flour	575 mL
1/2 cup	granulated sugar	125 mL
1 cup	butter	250 mL
1	egg, beaten	1
1/4 cup	coarse sugar	50 mL
1/3 cup	finely chopped unblanched almonds	75 mL

● In large bowl, stir flour with granulated sugar; using pastry blender or two knives, cut in butter until in fine crumbs. Gather into ball; knead lightly until smooth and dough holds together in ball.

● Divide dough into 6 portions. On lightly floured surface, roll each portion into 10-inch (25 cm) long log; flatten with knife to 1/2-inch (1 cm) thickness. Brush with egg; sprinkle with coarse sugar and almonds.

● Cut diagonally into 1-inch (2.5 cm) thick slices to form diamond shapes. Place on greased baking sheets. Bake in 325°F (160°C) oven for 10 to 12 minutes or until golden brown on edges. Makes about 54 cookies.

*F*innish "bread" is a misleading translation for these crunchy almond slices. This is just one of the traditional Danish treats that Birthe Marie Macdonald shows students how to make in her Brampton, Ontario, cooking school.

Per cookie: about
- 66 calories
- 1 g protein
- 4 g fat
- 7 g carbohydrate

TIP: Coarse granulated sugar is best for the crunchy topping. Look for it in delicatessens or bulk-food stores.

Macaroon Jam Slices ▲

A groove in an egg-white-and-ground-almond dough holds raspberry jam. After baking, cut this elegant confection on the diagonal into diamond-shaped slices. Other jams such as apricot, gooseberry, blackberry or marmalade can replace the raspberry.

Per cookie: about
- 86 calories
- 5 g fat
- 2 g protein
- 9 g carbohydrate

1	egg white	1
1/2 cup	icing sugar	125 mL
1/2 tsp	vanilla	2 mL
1-3/4 cups	ground almonds	425 mL
1/3 cup	raspberry jam	75 mL

● In large bowl, beat egg white until soft peaks form. Beat in 1/3 cup (75 mL) of the sugar, 2 tbsp (25 mL) at a time, until stiff peaks form. Fold in vanilla. Fold in all but 2 tbsp (25 mL) of the almonds.

● Divide dough in half. Dust work surface with half of the remaining sugar and half of the remaining almonds; roll one-half of the dough into 10-inch (25 cm) long log. Repeat with remaining sugar, almonds and dough.

● With two spatulas, place logs, 2 inches (5 cm) apart, on greased baking sheet. With fingertip, form groove lengthwise along center of each log to 1/4 inch (5 mm) of bottom, keeping walls about 1/4 inch (5 mm) thick to support filling.

● Bake in 350°F (180°C) oven for 10 minutes. Spoon raspberry jam into each groove. Bake for about 12 minutes or until cookie is golden and jam is bubbly. Let cool on pan on rack for 5 minutes. Cut diagonally into 1-inch (2.5 cm) thick slices. Makes about 18 cookies.

Sesame Wafers

1/2 cup	sesame seeds	125 mL
1 cup	butter, softened	250 mL
1 cup	packed brown sugar	250 mL
1-1/2 tsp	vanilla	7 mL
2-1/2 cups	all-purpose flour	625 mL
3/4 tsp	baking soda	4 mL
Pinch	salt	Pinch

● In skillet, toast sesame seeds over medium-high heat for about 3 minutes or until golden; set aside.

● In large bowl, beat butter with sugar until fluffy; beat in vanilla. In separate bowl, stir together flour, baking soda, salt and 1/4 cup (50 mL) of the sesame seeds. With wooden spoon, stir into butter mixture in two additions.

● Divide dough into thirds. Sprinkle one-third of the remaining sesame seeds onto large piece of waxed paper. Using paper as guide, roll one portion of the dough into 8-inch (20 cm) long log, coating with sesame seeds. Remove paper. Wrap in plastic wrap, twisting ends to seal.

● Repeat with remaining dough. Refrigerate for at least 3 hours or until firm. *(Logs can be refrigerated for up to 3 days or frozen for up to 3 weeks; thaw for 20 minutes.)*

● Cut into 1/4-inch (5 mm) thick slices; place, 2 inches (5 cm) apart, on greased baking sheets. Bake in 375°F (190°C) oven for 10 to 12 minutes or until light brown. Makes about 84 cookies.

VARIATION

● ALMOND WAFERS: Substitute 1/4 tsp (1 mL) almond extract for vanilla. Substitute 3/4 cup (175 mL) ground almonds for the sesame seeds, incorporating all in flour mixture. *(Logs can be refrigerated for up to 3 days or frozen for up to 2 weeks; thaw for 20 minutes.)* Cut 42 blanched almonds in half; place almond half on each cookie before baking for 10 to 15 minutes or until light golden.

These crisp morsels are sometimes called benne wafers, from an African word for sesame seeds. Be sure to try the almond variation, too.

Per cookie: about
- 50 calories
- 1 g protein
- 3 g fat
- 6 g carbohydrate

Crunchy Chocolate Wafers

3/4 cup	granulated sugar	175 mL
1/3 cup	butter, softened	75 mL
1	egg, lightly beaten	1
1 cup	all-purpose flour	250 mL
1/4 cup	unsweetened cocoa powder	50 mL
1/4 tsp	each cinnamon and salt	1 mL
2 oz	semisweet or white chocolate, coarsely chopped	60 g

● In large bowl, beat 1/2 cup (125 mL) of the sugar with butter until sugar is moistened; beat in egg. In separate bowl, sift together flour, cocoa, cinnamon and salt; add to butter mixture all at once, stirring with wooden spoon to make stiff dough.

● Shape rounded teaspoonfuls (5 mL) into balls; place, 2 inches (5 cm) apart, on parchment paper-lined or greased baking sheets. Dip base of lightly greased glass into remaining sugar; flatten balls to 1/8-inch (3 mm) thickness, sugaring glass after each cookie. Bake in 350°F (180°C) oven for about 12 minutes or until firm. Transfer to rack and let cool.

● In bowl over saucepan of hot (not boiling) water, melt chocolate, stirring occasionally; drizzle with fork over cooled cookies. Makes about 30 cookies.

These chocolate-drizzled treats are good cookie insurance — keep a tin of them on hand and serve with ice cream when unexpected guests drop in.

Per cookie: about
- 67 calories
- 1 g protein
- 3 g fat
- 10 g carbohydrate

Orange Pecan Crescents

Tender buttery nut crescents with a twist of orange are perfect for entertaining, especially at holiday time.

Per cookie: about
- 85 calories
- 1 g protein
- 6 g fat
- 6 g carbohydrate

1 cup	unsalted butter, softened	250 mL
1/2 cup	(approx) icing sugar	125 mL
2 tbsp	orange liqueur	25 mL
2 tsp	grated orange rind	10 mL
2 cups	all-purpose flour	500 mL
1/2 tsp	salt	2 mL
1-1/2 cups	finely chopped toasted pecans	375 mL

● In large bowl, beat butter until light; gradually beat in sugar until fluffy. Stir in liqueur and orange rind. Stir flour with salt; stir into butter mixture until blended. Stir in pecans.

● With lightly floured hands, shape rounded teaspoonfuls (5 mL) into crescents; place, 1 inch (2.5 cm) apart, on ungreased baking sheets. Bake in 325°F (160°C) oven for about 25 minutes or until light golden. Transfer to racks; dust lightly with more icing sugar. Makes 48 cookies.

Almond Pine Nut Crescents ▼

The tops of these ground almond crescents are crusted attractively with chopped pine nuts.

Per cookie: about
- 124 calories
- 3 g protein
- 9 g fat
- 11 g carbohydrate

1/2 cup	unsalted butter, softened	125 mL
1/2 cup	granulated sugar	125 mL
1	egg	1
2 tsp	grated orange rind	10 mL
1/2 tsp	almond extract	2 mL
1-1/4 cups	all-purpose flour	300 mL
1/2 cup	ground almonds	125 mL
1 tsp	baking powder	5 mL
1 cup	pine nuts, coarsely chopped	250 mL

● In large bowl, beat butter with sugar until light and fluffy. Beat in egg, orange rind and almond extract until smooth. In separate bowl, stir together flour, almonds and baking powder; stir into butter mixture just until moistened. Cover and refrigerate for 30 minutes or until chilled and firm.

● Spread pine nuts in shallow dish. With moistened hands, shape tablespoonfuls (15 mL) into crescents. Press tops firmly into nuts to adhere. Place, about 2 inches (5 cm) apart, on greased baking sheets; bake in 350°F (180°C) oven for 12 to 15 minutes or until golden. Makes 24 cookies.

TIP: For a change of taste, try grated lemon rind instead of orange.

Almond Pine Nut Crescents (right) and Cranberry Crumble Squares (p. 71)

INVITE FRIENDS TO A COOKIE-BAKING PARTY

Next time you need cookies for a bazaar or bake sale, invite friends to share the baking — and the fun.

● Choose a day convenient for all, keeping in mind the maximum time indicated for storing the cookies.

● Shape-and-bake cookies are a good idea because whole rolls can be frozen and used when needed, or nicely packaged as a gift.

● Request that each person bring a large bowl and set of beaters.

● Measure ingredients before guests arrive, if possible. If you are not premeasuring, set out the flour, sugar, butter, eggs, baking powder and baking soda in a central location, with dry measures and spoons nearby. Several bowls will be needed to hold measured ingredients.

● Be sure to supply a variety of add-ins, such as mini chocolate and butterscotch chips, toffee pieces and chopped nuts. Provide sprinkles and coarse sugar in seasonal colors for those who want to roll the dough in them, as well as white and bittersweet chocolate for dipping or drizzling.

● Take the butter out of the refrigerator before the gathering to ensure that it's soft enough to beat easily.

● Divide your kitchen into "stations," with a maximum of two people at each.

● Stations must be close to electrical outlets so that everyone can use electric beaters or food processors.

● Have plenty of waxed paper and plastic wrap on hand. Colored cellophane or plastic wrap for packaging adds to the spirit of the occasion.

● Advise guests to use lightly greased cookie sheets (no sides) rather than rimmed baking sheets (jelly roll pans) for even baking. Remember that cookies bake slightly faster on dark sheets than on light ones.

● Bake a few of the cookies ahead of time for sampling and snacking — rewards for everyone's hard work.

Crystal Lemon Drops

1-1/4 cups	granulated sugar	300 mL
3 tbsp	butter, softened	50 mL
2	egg whites	2
1 tbsp	grated lemon rind	15 mL
2 tbsp	lemon juice	25 mL
1 tsp	vanilla	5 mL
1-1/2 cups	all-purpose flour	375 mL
1/2 cup	cornmeal	125 mL
1/4 tsp	each baking soda and salt	1 mL

● In large bowl, beat 1 cup (250 mL) of the sugar with butter until sugar is moistened; beat in egg whites. Beat in lemon rind, lemon juice and vanilla. In separate bowl, stir together flour, cornmeal, baking soda and salt; stir into sugar mixture all at once.

● Shape rounded teaspoonfuls (5 mL) into balls; place, 2 inches (5 cm) apart, on parchment paper-lined or greased baking sheets. Dip base of lightly greased glass into remaining sugar; flatten balls to 1/4-inch (5 mm) thickness, sugaring glass after each cookie. Bake in 350°F (180°C) oven for about 12 minutes or until edges are light golden. Makes 48 cookies.

W*e've cut back on the butter but not on the great taste of these crunchy drops. Enjoy them with a glass of milk, a cup of tea or your favorite fruit dessert.*

Per cookie: about
● 50 calories   ● 1 g protein
● 1 g fat   ● 9 g carbohydrate

Sugar Dusties

Known as polvorones in Mexico, these buttery shortbread bites are rolled in sugar and cinnamon.

Per cookie: about
- 89 calories
- 4 g fat
- 1 g protein
- 8 g carbohydrate

3/4 cup	butter, softened	175 mL
1/2 cup	icing sugar	125 mL
1	egg yolk	1
1 tsp	vanilla	5 mL
1-3/4 cups	all-purpose flour	425 mL
1 tsp	cinnamon	5 mL
1/2 tsp	baking powder	2 mL
	SUGAR COATING	
1/4 cup	granulated sugar	50 mL
1/4 tsp	cinnamon	1 mL

● In large bowl, beat butter with sugar until light and fluffy; beat in egg yolk and vanilla. In separate bowl, stir together flour, cinnamon and baking powder; gradually stir into butter mixture.

● Shape into 1-inch (2.5 cm) balls; place, 1 inch (2.5 cm) apart, on ungreased baking sheets. Bake in 350°F (180°C) oven for 17 to 20 minutes or just until starting to turn golden.

● SUGAR COATING: In shallow dish, combine sugar and cinnamon. Gently roll warm cookies in sugar mixture until well coated. Makes about 36 cookies.

Sugared Chocolate Fingers

These chocolate and nut cookies, of Greek inspiration, are exceptionally tender and rich. Include them in any special-occasion cookie platter.

Per cookie: about
- 91 calories
- 6 g fat
- 1 g protein
- 10 g carbohydrate

1/3 cup	toasted pecans	75 mL
2/3 cup	icing sugar	150 mL
1 tbsp	unsweetened cocoa powder	15 mL
1 tsp	instant coffee granules (optional)	5 mL
3/4 cup	butter, softened	175 mL
2	egg yolks	2
1 tsp	vanilla	5 mL
2 oz	bittersweet chocolate, finely grated	60 g
2 cups	all-purpose flour	500 mL
	TOPPING	
1/4 cup	granulated sugar	50 mL
2 tsp	unsweetened cocoa powder	10 mL

● In food processor, grind pecans with icing sugar until very fine. In small bowl, whisk together cocoa, coffee granules (if using) and 1 tbsp (15 mL) hot water; set aside.

● In large bowl, beat butter with pecan mixture for about 4 minutes or until light. Beat in egg yolks; beat in cocoa mixture, vanilla and grated chocolate. Stir in flour, in four additions, to form moist dough. Cover and refrigerate for 30 minutes. *(Dough can be refrigerated for up to 24 hours; let stand at room temperature for 30 minutes.)*

● Shape tablespoonfuls (15 mL) into 2-1/2-inch (6 cm) long fingers; place, 2 inches (5 cm) apart, on greased baking sheets. Bake in 350°F (180°C) oven for about 15 minutes or until firm to the touch. Let cool on pan on rack for 5 minutes.

● TOPPING: In shallow dish, combine sugar with cocoa; roll cookies in mixture to coat. Makes 36 cookies.

Melomakarona

2	eggs, separated	2
2/3 cup	butter, softened	150 mL
2/3 cup	shortening	150 mL
2/3 cup	granulated sugar	150 mL
1 tbsp	brandy	15 mL
1 tsp	each grated orange and lemon rind	5 mL
1 tsp	vanilla	5 mL
3-1/2 cups	sifted cake-and-pastry flour	875 mL
2 tsp	baking powder	10 mL
1-1/2 tsp	cinnamon	7 mL
1/2 tsp	ground cloves	2 mL

SYRUP		
1-1/2 cups	mild liquid honey	375 mL
1 cup	water	250 mL
1/2 cup	granulated sugar	125 mL
1	each strip orange and lemon rind	1

GARNISH		
1 cup	(approx) liquid honey	250 mL
1-1/2 cups	finely chopped walnuts	375 mL
	Whole cloves (optional)	

● In bowl, beat egg whites until stiff peaks form; set aside. In large bowl, beat together butter, shortening and sugar until light and fluffy; beat in egg yolks in two additions. Blend in brandy, orange and lemon rinds and vanilla. Fold in beaten whites. In separate bowl, stir together flour, baking powder, cinnamon and cloves; gradually stir into egg mixture until combined.

● Turn out onto well-floured surface (dough will be sticky); knead lightly 10 times. Form into disc; wrap in plastic wrap and refrigerate for 1 hour.

● With floured fingertips, roll tablespoonfuls (15 mL) into 2-inch (5 cm) long fingers; place, 2 inches (5 cm) apart, on greased baking sheets. Bake in 350°F (180°C) oven for 25 to 30 minutes or until golden. Let cool on racks.

● SYRUP: In small saucepan, bring honey, water, sugar and orange and lemon rinds to boil, stirring frequently to dissolve sugar. Reduce heat to medium; simmer, without stirring, for 10 minutes or until slightly thickened. Keep warm over low heat.

● Slide baking sheets under racks with cookies to catch any drips. Immerse about 6 cookies at a time into warm syrup for 30 seconds. Using slotted spoon, return cookies to rack.

● GARNISH: Spoon about 1 tsp (5 mL) honey over each cookie; sprinkle immediately with walnuts. Stud center of each with whole clove (if using). Sprinkle with any remaining honey and nuts. Store in rigid airtight container for at least 1 day or for up to 1 week. Makes about 54 cookies.

*C*elebrating Easter in the Greek community means special sweets, including these nutty spice cookies drenched in honey syrup. Although the cookies take a bit of time to make, they keep well and taste better once they've had a day to mellow.

Per cookie: about
- 149 calories
- 1 g protein
- 7 g fat
- 21 g carbohydrate

TIP: For an impressive presentation, stack cookies in a multi-tiered mound on a pedestal serving plate.

Pecan Snowballs

With a coating of white icing sugar and toasted pecan flavor in every bite, these luscious little morsels will just melt in your mouth.

Per cookie: about
- 116 calories
- 1 g protein
- 9 g fat
- 9 g carbohydrate

1 cup	butter, softened	250 mL
1-1/4 cups	icing sugar	300 mL
1-1/2 tsp	vanilla	7 mL
2 cups	all-purpose flour	500 mL
2 cups	pecans, toasted and finely chopped (see p.12)	500 mL
1/2 tsp	salt	2 mL

● In large bowl, beat butter with 1/4 cup (50 mL) of the sugar until smooth; beat in vanilla. With wooden spoon, stir in flour, nuts and salt, using hands to finish mixing and form dough into ball. Wrap in plastic wrap; refrigerate for 30 minutes.

● Shape into 1-inch (2.5 cm) balls; place, 1 inch (2.5 cm) apart, on ungreased baking sheets. Bake in 325°F (160°C) oven for 18 to 20 minutes or until lightly golden. Transfer to racks and let cool for 5 minutes.

● Roll balls in remaining sugar; let cool completely on rack. Roll again in sugar. Makes about 40 cookies.

Coconut Cookies

Vancouver chef Karen Barnaby created this recipe to celebrate the flavors of Hawaii. Serve with fruit sorbet, ice cream or custard pudding.

Per cookie: about
- 145 calories
- 1 g protein
- 10 g fat
- 13 g carbohydrate

1-1/4 cups	butter, softened	300 mL
1 cup	granulated sugar	250 mL
1	egg yolk	1
2-1/4 cups	all-purpose flour	550 mL
2 cups	unsweetened medium-shred coconut	500 mL
Pinch	nutmeg	Pinch

● In large bowl, beat butter until creamy; beat in sugar until smooth. Beat in egg yolk until slightly fluffy. With wooden spoon, stir in flour, coconut and nutmeg until combined. Wrap dough in plastic wrap; chill until firm, about 2 hours.

● Roll heaping tablespoonfuls (15 mL) into 3-inch (8 cm) long fingers. Place, 2 inches (5 cm) apart, on greased and floured or parchment paper-lined baking sheets; flatten with fork to 1/4-inch (5 mm) thickness. Refrigerate for 30 minutes.

● Bake in 325°F (160°C) oven for 25 to 30 minutes or until golden around edges. Makes 36 cookies.

Snickerdoodles

This nonsensical name belongs to a down-home cookie of East Coast origin — a crispy mound with a light interior, whole-nut topping and cinnamon-sugar coating. Fill your cookie jar with a batch, and be prepared for reorders.

Per cookie: about
- 87 calories
- 1 g protein
- 4 g fat
- 11 g carbohydrate

1/2 cup	butter, softened	125 mL
3/4 cup	granulated sugar	175 mL
1	egg	1
1 tsp	vanilla	5 mL
1-1/2 cups	all-purpose flour	375 mL
1 tsp	baking powder	5 mL
Pinch	salt	Pinch
	TOPPING	
3 tbsp	granulated sugar	50 mL
2 tsp	cinnamon	10 mL
30	pecan halves	30

● In large bowl, beat butter with sugar until light and fluffy; beat in egg and vanilla. In separate bowl, stir together flour, baking powder and salt; stir into butter mixture.

● TOPPING: On small plate, stir sugar with cinnamon. Shape dough into 1-inch (2.5 cm) balls; roll in sugar mixture to coat. Lightly press pecan on top of each.

● Place, 2 inches (5 cm) apart, on greased baking sheets. Bake in 350°F (180°C) oven for about 15 minutes or until golden brown around edges. Makes 30 cookies.

Fat Teddies ▼

1/2 cup	butter, softened	125 mL
1 cup	packed brown sugar	250 mL
1/2 cup	smooth peanut butter	125 mL
1/2 tsp	vanilla	2 mL
1	egg	1
2 oz	semisweet chocolate, melted	60 g
2 cups	all-purpose flour	500 mL
1/2 tsp	baking soda	2 mL
	Raisins or currants (optional)	

● In large bowl, beat together butter, sugar, peanut butter and vanilla until smooth. Beat in egg, beating well. Transfer about 1 cup (250 mL) to separate bowl; combine with melted chocolate.

● Stir 1 cup (250 mL) of the flour with 1/4 tsp (1 mL) of the baking soda; gradually add to chocolate batter, blending thoroughly. Add remaining flour and baking soda to plain batter, blending thoroughly.

● Working with small pieces of dough at a time and keeping remainder covered with plastic wrap, shape 1-inch (2.5 cm) balls for bodies and heads; press together. Place, 2 inches (5 cm) apart, on greased baking sheets; press lightly to flatten.

● Shape and add small bits of dough for ears, arms and legs, pressing together. Add raisins (if using) or tiny bits of contrasting dough for eyes, mouth, buttons and paws. Cover with plastic wrap and refrigerate for 30 minutes.

● Bake in 350°F (180°C) oven for 12 to 15 minutes or until firm to the touch and lightly browned. Makes about 16 cookies.

From the creative kitchen of food writer Margaret Fraser comes this delightful idea for a family cookie project. Mix and match the two doughs to form arms, legs, ears and bodies.

Per cookie: about
● 229 calories
● 12 g fat
● 4 g protein
● 29 g carbohydrate

Bachelor Buttons

1 cup	butter, softened	250 mL
1/2 cup	granulated sugar	125 mL
2	egg yolks	2
2 tsp	vanilla	10 mL
2 cups	all-purpose flour	500 mL
2	egg whites, lightly beaten	2
1/3 cup	shredded coconut or finely chopped nuts	75 mL
1/2 cup	jelly or jam	125 mL

● In large bowl, beat butter with sugar until light; beat in egg yolks and vanilla. Gradually stir in flour.

● Shape into 1-inch (2.5 cm) balls; dip into egg whites and roll in coconut. Place, 2 inches (5 cm) apart, on greased baking sheets. With wooden spoon handle, make depression in center of each cookie. Bake in 325°F (160°C) oven for 10 to 12 minutes or just until firm. Fill depressions with jelly. Makes about 48 cookies.

VARIATION

● BROWN-EYED SUSANS: Fill centers of just-baked cookies with 2 or 3 chocolate chips — they'll melt from the warmth of the cookie.

This old-time classic is a variation on a thimble cookie, which has a jam-filled depression in the center.

Per cookie: about
● 76 calories
● 4 g fat
● 1 g protein
● 9 g carbohydrate

Oatmeal Date Sandwich Cookies ▲

Whether you eat them on their own as oatmeal cookies or sandwich them together with a thick date filling, you won't find a better version of a great Canadian classic.

Per cookie: about
- 334 calories
- 12 g fat
- high source of fiber
- 4 g protein
- 56 g carbohydrate

2/3 cup	butter, softened	150 mL
1 cup	packed brown sugar	250 mL
1	egg	1
1 tbsp	vanilla	15 mL
1-1/2 cups	rolled oats (not instant)	375 mL
1 cup	all-purpose flour	250 mL
1/2 tsp	each baking powder and baking soda	2 mL
1/4 tsp	salt	1 mL
2 cups	pitted dates, chopped	500 mL
1 tbsp	grated orange rind	15 mL
2/3 cup	orange juice	150 mL

● In large bowl, beat butter with sugar until fluffy; beat in egg and vanilla. In separate bowl, stir together rolled oats, flour, baking powder, baking soda and salt; gradually stir into butter mixture until blended. Cover with plastic wrap and refrigerate for at least 30 minutes or for up to 1 day.

● Meanwhile, in small heavy saucepan, bring dates, orange rind, orange juice and 1/3 cup (75 mL) water to boil over medium heat, stirring often. Reduce heat to low; cover and simmer, stirring occasionally, for about 45 minutes or until dates are very soft. Uncover and cook, stirring constantly, for 5 minutes or until thickened and sticky. Let cool completely. *(Filling can be covered and refrigerated for up to 2 days.)*

● Shape heaping tablespoonfuls (15 mL) into 24 balls. Place, 2 inches (5 cm) apart, on greased baking sheets. Bake in 350°F (180°C) oven for 12 to 15 minutes or until golden, edges are crispy and centers are still soft. Transfer cookies immediately to rack. Let cool completely.

● Spread date purée evenly over smooth side of 12 of the cookies; sandwich with remaining cookies, smooth side down. Makes 12 large cookies.

TIP: When making the cookies and not the filling, feel free to play with add-ins. Currants, raisins, toasted nuts, white and dark chocolate, peanut butter chips, toffee chips and dried cranberries are all delicious. Use up to 1 cup (250 mL).

Ginger Crinkles

2/3 cup	vegetable oil	150 mL
1-1/4 cups	granulated sugar	300 mL
1	egg	1
1/4 cup	fancy molasses	50 mL
1-3/4 cups	all-purpose flour	425 mL
2 tsp	ground ginger	10 mL
1 tsp	cinnamon	5 mL
1 tsp	each baking powder and baking soda	5 mL
1/2 tsp	salt	2 mL

● In large bowl, whisk oil with 1 cup (250 mL) of the sugar; whisk in egg until smooth. Whisk in molasses. In separate bowl, stir together flour, ginger, cinnamon, baking powder, baking soda and salt; stir into molasses mixture to form moist dough.

● Shape tablespoonfuls (15 mL) into balls; roll in remaining sugar to coat. Place, 2 inches (5 cm) apart, on greased baking sheets. Bake in 375°F (190°C) oven for about 12 minutes or until flattened, cracked and browned all over. Makes 36 cookies.

Thanks go to Calgarian Julie Parsons for this fine version of one of Canada's most popular cookies. The balls of cookie dough, rolled in sugar, spread as they bake, forming a characteristic "cracked" or crinkled surface.

Per cookie: about
- 95 calories
- 1 g protein
- 4 g fat
- 13 g carbohydrate

TIP: For a flatter, crispier cookie without cracks, use a fork to press down balls of dough on baking sheet before baking.

Brandy Balls

3 oz	semisweet chocolate, coarsely chopped	90 g
1/2 cup	granulated sugar	125 mL
1/3 cup	brandy or rum	75 mL
1/4 cup	corn syrup	50 mL
2-1/2 cups	finely crushed vanilla wafers	625 mL
3/4 cup	finely chopped pecans or walnuts	175 mL
3/4 cup	mixed candied fruit or chopped crystallized ginger (optional)	175 mL
	COATING	
1/3 cup	granulated sugar	75 mL

● In large bowl over saucepan of hot (not boiling) water, melt chocolate, stirring occasionally; stir in sugar, brandy and syrup. Stir in wafer crumbs, nuts, and fruit (if using), mixing thoroughly. Chill until firm.

● COATING: Shape into 1-inch (2.5 cm) balls; roll in sugar.

● Layer between waxed paper in airtight container and store in cool, dry place (not refrigerator) for a few days before serving. Makes about 50 balls.

Create an assortment of these easy no-bake treats by rolling balls in different coatings — icing sugar, cocoa, coconut or very finely chopped nuts — or pressing a candied cherry or nut half into some of them.

Per ball: about
- 60 calories
- trace protein
- 2 g fat
- 9 g carbohydrate

TIP: To make rum balls, substitute chocolate wafers for the vanilla, and rum for the brandy.

Rolled or Pressed Cookies

Rolling out or pressing cookies is a rite of passage for cookie makers. Now, all sorts of beautifully shaped cookies are possible — from gingerbread tree ornaments and cinnamon stars to sugar-cookie hearts, meringue wreaths and fruity rugulahs.

Sugar Cookies ▶

Baking sugar cookies is the perfect way to get everyone in the family together in the kitchen. With an easy-to-handle dough, it takes no time to cut sugar cookies into interesting shapes to suit any season or occasion. This leaves plenty of time for the real fun — icing and decorating!

Per cookie: about
- 89 calories
- 4 g fat
- 1 g protein
- 12 g carbohydrate

3/4 cup	butter, softened	175 mL
1 cup	granulated or packed brown sugar	250 mL
1	egg	1
1 tsp	vanilla	5 mL
2-1/2 cups	all-purpose flour	625 mL
1/2 tsp	baking powder	2 mL
Pinch	salt	Pinch

● In large bowl, beat butter until light and fluffy; beat in sugar in three additions. Beat in egg and vanilla. In separate bowl, stir together flour, baking powder and salt; with wooden spoon, stir into butter mixture in three additions.

● Divide dough in half; flatten slightly. Wrap each half in plastic wrap; refrigerate for at least 1 hour or for up to 24 hours.

● On lightly floured surface, roll out each half to 1/4-inch (5 mm) thickness. Using 3-inch (8 cm) cookie cutter, cut out shapes. Place, 1 inch (2.5 cm) apart, on parchment paper-lined or greased baking sheets.

● Bake in 375°F (190°C) oven for about 10 minutes or until light golden on bottom and edges. Decorate as desired (see pages 40 and 42). Makes 36 cookies.

DECORATING COOKIES

● Bulk food stores are ideal for choosing decorating material for cookies. You can buy more kinds for less money and in small amounts so you don't have awkward leftovers.

● Decorating cookies is a great party idea for birthdays, Christmas, Halloween and other events. Let kids help with choosing just the right candies.

FINISHING TOUCHES

Use the recipe for Sugar Cookies (previous page) as the basis for these delightful cookie extravaganzas.

COOKIE WANDS

● Use 3-inch (8 cm) star cookie cutter to cut out shapes. Place marble-size piece of dough on parchment paper-lined or greased baking sheet. Press lollipop stick or wooden craft stick into dough. Place star cookie cutout over top, pressing lightly to stick dough together. Sprinkle with gold dust. Bake as directed.

JAM-FILLED COOKIES

● Use 3-inch (8 cm) star cookie cutter to cut out shapes. Use mini cutter to cut hole in center of half of the unbaked cookies for tops. Bake as directed.
● Spread about 1/2 tsp (2 mL) raspberry jam over middle of each whole cookie. Dust tops with icing sugar; place over jam. For 18 cookies, you need about 1/3 cup (75 mL) jam.

STAINED GLASS COOKIES

● Use 3-inch (8 cm) cookie cutter to cut out shapes. Use mini cutter for cutouts. Place on parchment paper-lined or greased foil-lined baking sheet. Separating colors, crush 1/3 cup (75 mL) clear hard candies. Spoon into holes, mounding slightly. Bake as directed; let cool on pan for 5 minutes. Transfer to rack; let cool completely to let candy harden.

Sugar and Spice Cookies ▼

1/2 cup	butter, softened	125 mL
1 cup	packed brown sugar	250 mL
1	egg	1
1/2 tsp	vanilla	2 mL
1-3/4 cups	all-purpose flour	425 mL
1 tsp	baking powder	5 mL
1 tsp	cinnamon	5 mL
1/4 tsp	ground nutmeg	1 mL
Pinch	ground cloves	Pinch

● In large bowl, beat butter with sugar until smooth; beat in egg and vanilla. In separate bowl, stir together flour, baking powder, cinnamon, nutmeg and cloves; stir into butter mixture until blended. Gather dough into ball; wrap and refrigerate for at least 1 hour or for up to 3 days.

● On lightly floured surface, roll out dough to 1/8-inch (3 mm) thickness. Using 2-inch (5 cm) cookie cutter, cut out rounds or desired shapes. Place, about 2 inches (5 cm) apart, on greased baking sheets. Bake in 350°F (180°C) oven for 10 to 12 minutes or just until edges begin to brown. Makes about 50 cookies.

A *mild spice cookie is a delicious variation on sugar cookies and offers just as many creative opportunities with cookie cutters, icings, candies, mini marshmallows and sprinkles (see box, p. 42).*

Per cookie: about
- 50 calories
- 1 g protein
- 2 g fat
- 8 g carbohydrate

THE ICING ON THE COOKIE

Use these easy icing recipes to decorate Sugar Cookies (p. 38), Sugar and Spice Cookies or any other cookie your heart desires. Cover icings with damp cloth or plastic wrap to prevent drying out. Refrigerate for up to 24 hours. Divide and tint with paste or liquid food coloring, if you like.

Piping Icing

● In bowl and using electric mixer, beat 2 tbsp (25 mL) meringue powder with 1/4 cup (50 mL) water. Slowly beat in 2-1/3 cups (575 mL) icing sugar until stiff, about 4 minutes. Makes 1-1/2 cups (375 mL).

Icing Paint

● In bowl, whisk 4 cups (1 L) icing sugar with 1/3 cup (75 mL) water, adding up to 2 tbsp (25 mL) more water if necessary to make spreadable. Makes 1-1/2 cups (375 mL).

DECORATOR SUGAR COOKIES

Use these icing ideas to transform Sugar Cookies (p. 38) or Sugar and Spice Cookies (p. 41) into spectacular treats.

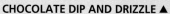

PIPING AND CANDIES ▼

● Divide and tint Piping Icing (recipe, p. 41) to use over dried base color. Spoon into piping bag fitted with plain tip; twist over icing. Holding bag at twist, squeeze out icing with slow even pressure, holding tip between thumb and forefinger to guide flow of icing. Press sprinkles or candies into icing while still moist.

CHOCOLATE DIP AND DRIZZLE ▲

● Dip cookie halfway into 6 oz (175 g) melted semisweet chocolate; scrape bottom against rim of rim of bowl to remove excess. Place on waxed paper-lined baking sheet. Dip fork into 3 oz (90 g) melted white or milk chocolate; drizzle over cookie with back-and-forth motion.

WEBBING ▲

● Coat cookie with melted chocolate or Icing Paint (recipe, p. 41). While first coat is still wet, pipe on stripes in contrasting color of chocolate, Icing Paint or Piping Icing (recipe, p. 41). Lightly drag toothpick or tip of small knife crosswise in straight lines through stripes.

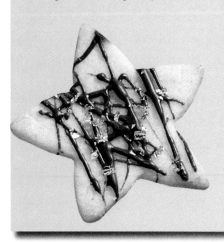

PAINTING ▲

● Divide and tint Icing Paint (recipe, p. 41). Using small paintbrushes or wooden craft sticks, paint on base color. Let dry completely before adding details in other colors. For less distinct, softer edges (as in green tree), paint on details while first coat is wet.

Gingerbread Cookies

1/2 cup	shortening	125 mL
1/2 cup	granulated sugar	125 mL
1	egg	1
1/3 cup	fancy molasses	75 mL
1/4 cup	blackstrap molasses	50 mL
2-3/4 cups	all-purpose flour	675 mL
1 tsp	ground ginger	5 mL
1/2 tsp	each baking soda, salt, cloves and cinnamon	2 mL

● In large bowl, beat shortening with sugar until fluffy; beat in egg and fancy and blackstrap molasses.

● Stir together flour, ginger, baking soda, salt, cloves and cinnamon; with wooden spoon, stir into molasses mixture in 3 additions until well combined, using hands when mixture becomes too stiff to stir.

● Gather into ball. Divide in half; flatten into discs. Wrap each in plastic wrap; refrigerate for at least 1 hour or until firm.

● Between sheets of waxed paper, roll out each portion of dough to 1/3-inch (3 mm) thickness. Remove top sheet of paper. Using 3-inch (8 cm) cookie cutter, cut out desired shapes, rerolling scraps once. Transfer to parchment paper-lined or greased baking sheets. Freeze for 20 minutes or until firm.

● Bake in 325°F (160°C) oven for 12 to 15 minutes or until golden and firm to the touch. Makes about 60 cookies.

TIP: Use this dough for gingerbread girls and boys or for angels, stars and Santas to string on the Christmas tree.

This is Canadian Living's favorite gingerbread cookie recipe. The balance of spices and the two kinds of molasses give these cookies a most appealing taste that does not fade, even when the cookies are several weeks old.

Per cookie: about
- 76 calories
- 3 g fat
- 1 g protein
- 12 g carbohydrate

Nannie's Molasses Cookies

1 cup	shortening	250 mL
1 cup	granulated sugar	250 mL
1 cup	fancy molasses	250 mL
1 tsp	each baking soda and salt	5 mL
1 tsp	each ground ginger, cinnamon, allspice and nutmeg	5 mL
3-1/2 cups	all-purpose flour	875 mL
1/2 cup	milk	125 mL

● In large bowl, beat shortening with sugar; beat in molasses, baking soda, salt, ginger, cinnamon, allspice and nutmeg. Mix in flour alternately with milk, making three additions of flour and two of milk. Form into ball; wrap and refrigerate for 4 hours.

● Divide in half. On lightly floured surface, roll out each half to 1/4-inch (5 mm) thickness. Using 2-1/2-inch (6 cm) round cookie cutter, cut out shapes; place, 2 inches (5 cm) apart, on greased baking sheets. Bake in 350°F (180°C) oven for 15 minutes or until edges are golden brown. Makes about 48 cookies.

Newfoundlander Jude Billard contributed her grandmother's cookie specialty to Canadian Living's 20th anniversary celebrations.

Per cookie: about
- 105 calories
- 4 g fat
- 1 g protein
- 16 g carbohydrate

Danish Twists

Anyone who has tasted these sugar-dusted, deep-fried strips of sweet dough knows they're worth every minute of effort — even as they melt away in your mouth! We guarantee you'll find them irresistible.

Per cookie: about
- 30 calories
- trace protein
- 2 g fat
- 4 g carbohydrate

2 cups	all-purpose flour	500 mL
1/3 cup	granulated sugar	75 mL
1 tbsp	finely grated lemon rind	15 mL
2 tsp	ground cardamom	10 mL
1/4 tsp	baking powder	1 mL
1/3 cup	butter	75 mL
2	eggs	2
2 tbsp	milk	25 mL
	Vegetable oil for deep-frying	
1/3 cup	icing sugar	75 mL

● In large bowl, stir together flour, sugar, lemon rind, cardamom and baking powder. Using pastry blender or two knives, cut in butter until in fine crumbs. In small bowl, beat eggs; blend in milk. With fork, stir into flour mixture until dough holds together. Gather into ball; knead until smooth.

● Divide into quarters. On lightly floured surface, roll out each portion to 1/8-inch (3 mm) thick 8- x 6-inch (20 x 15 cm) rectangle; cut into 4- x 1-1/2-inch (10 x 4 cm) strips. Make 1-inch (2.5 cm) slit in center of each strip; twist 1 end through hole loosely. Set aside on floured baking sheet.

● In deep-fryer, heat oil to 350°F (180°C). Deep-fry a few twists at a time, turning once, for about 2 minutes or until golden brown. Remove to paper towels to drain and let cool; dust with icing sugar. Serve immediately. Makes about 84 cookies.

TIP: If you don't have a deep-frying thermometer, use a 1-inch (2.5 cm) cube of white bread instead. Drop bread into heated oil; the oil temperature is correct when bread turns golden brown in 65 seconds.

Empire Cookies

These iced and jam-filled buttery cookie sandwiches are a favorite on Scottish and English tea tables. Judging by the frequent calls to the Test Kitchen for this recipe, they're a favorite across Canada, too.

Per cookie: about
- 124 calories
- 1 g protein
- 4 g fat
- 21 g carbohydrate

1/2 cup	butter, softened	125 mL
1/2 cup	granulated sugar	125 mL
1	egg	1
1 tsp	vanilla	5 mL
2 cups	all-purpose flour	500 mL
1 tsp	baking powder	5 mL
1/3 cup	raspberry jam	75 mL
1 cup	sifted icing sugar	250 mL
1/4 tsp	almond extract	1 mL
1 tbsp	(approx) hot water	15 mL
24	pieces candied cherry	24

● In large bowl, beat butter until light; beat in granulated sugar. Beat in egg and vanilla. Mix flour with baking powder; gradually stir into butter mixture.

● On lightly floured surface, roll out dough to 1/8-inch (3 mm) thickness. Using 2-inch (5 cm) round cookie cutter, cut out shapes; place, 2 inches (5 cm) apart, on ungreased baking sheets. Bake in 350°F (180°C) oven for about 10 minutes or until very lightly browned at edges. Let cool completely.

● Spread half of the cookies with jam; top with remaining cookies. In small bowl, combine icing sugar, almond extract and enough hot water to make thin icing; spread over tops of cookies. Top each with cherry piece. Makes about 24 cookies.

Speculaas ▼

1/2 cup	butter, softened	125 mL
1 cup	packed brown sugar	250 mL
1	egg	1
1 cup	all-purpose flour	250 mL
3/4 cup	whole wheat flour	175 mL
2 tsp	each cinnamon and ground ginger	10 mL
1/2 tsp	each baking powder, baking soda and allspice	2 mL
1/4 tsp	each ground cardamom, cloves and nutmeg	1 mL
1/4 tsp	each salt and pepper	1 mL
1 tbsp	milk	15 mL
1/2 cup	sliced almonds	125 mL

● In large bowl, beat butter with sugar until fluffy; beat in egg. In separate bowl, stir together all-purpose and whole wheat flours, cinnamon, ginger, baking powder, baking soda, allspice, cardamom, cloves, nutmeg, salt and pepper; using wooden spoon, gradually stir into butter mixture.

● On lightly floured surface, gather dough into ball and knead 10 times; flatten into disc. Wrap in plastic wrap; refrigerate for 30 minutes.

● On lightly floured surface, roll out dough to 1/4-inch (5 mm) thickness. Cut into 3- x 2-inch (8 x 5 cm) rectangles or, using cookie cutter, into other desired shapes; place, 1/2 inch (1 cm) apart, on greased baking sheets. Brush with milk; press almonds decoratively into tops.

● Bake in 350°F (180°C) oven for 8 to 10 minutes or until edges darken slightly and tops are firm. Makes about 28 cookies.

T est kitchen assistant Susan Van Hezewijk delved into her Dutch heritage to bake this easier roll-and-cut version of spice cookies traditionally moulded in carved wooden boards.

Per cookie: about
• 101 calories   • 2 g protein
• 5 g fat   • 14 g carbohydrate

The name "speculaas" comes from the Latin speculum *(looking glass), because the cookies reflect the carved moulds.*

English Currant Cookies

From the Victorian era come these pretty cookies that you can cut out in crinkle-edged rounds or other fanciful shapes. Leave them plain for everyday pleasure or make them special-occasion with a dusting of icing sugar.

Per cookie: about
- 42 calories
- 1 g protein
- 2 g fat
- 5 g carbohydrate

1/2 cup	butter, softened	125 mL
3/4 cup	icing sugar, sifted	175 mL
1	egg	1
1 tsp	grated lemon rind	5 mL
1/2 tsp	vanilla	2 mL
1-1/2 cups	all-purpose flour	375 mL
1/2 tsp	baking powder	2 mL
1/2 tsp	grated nutmeg	2 mL
1/3 cup	dried currants	75 mL

● In large bowl, beat butter with sugar until fluffy; beat in egg, lemon rind and vanilla. In separate bowl, stir together flour, baking powder and nutmeg; stir into butter mixture in three additions. Stir in currants.

● Gather into ball; flatten into disc. Wrap in plastic wrap; refrigerate for at least 1 hour or until chilled. *(Dough can be refrigerated for up to 3 days.)*

● On lightly floured surface, roll out dough to 1/8-inch (3 mm) thickness. Using 2-inch (5 cm) round cookie cutter, cut out shapes; place, 2 inches (5 cm) apart, on ungreased baking sheets. Bake in 350°F (180°C) oven for about 12 minutes or until light golden. Makes about 48 cookies.

Milan Sandwich Cookies

The orange-flavored sandwich cookies known as biscotti Milano in Italy mirror the sophistication of the city for which they are named.

Per cookie: about
- 137 calories
- 1 g protein
- 9 g fat
- 13 g carbohydrate

1 tsp	vanilla	5 mL
1/2 tsp	instant espresso powder or instant coffee granules	2 mL
3/4 cup	butter, softened	175 mL
2/3 cup	granulated sugar	150 mL
1	egg	1
2 tsp	finely grated orange rind	10 mL
1-1/4 cups	all-purpose flour	300 mL
1/4 tsp	baking powder	1 mL
	CHOCOLATE GLAZE	
4 oz	semisweet chocolate, coarsely chopped	125 g
3 tbsp	butter	50 mL
1/4 tsp	instant espresso powder or instant coffee granules	1 mL

● In small bowl, stir vanilla with espresso powder; set aside.

● In large bowl, beat butter with sugar until light and fluffy; beat in egg, orange rind and vanilla mixture. In separate bowl, stir flour with baking powder; using wooden spoon, gradually stir into butter mixture.

● Using pastry bag fitted with small plain tip, pipe dough into 1-1/2-inch (4 cm) long strips, about 3 inches (8 cm) apart, onto greased baking sheets.

● Bake in 375°F (190°C) oven for 8 to 9 minutes or until golden brown around edges. Transfer to rack; let cool. *(Cookies can be layered between waxed paper in airtight container and frozen for up to 2 weeks.)*

● CHOCOLATE GLAZE: In bowl over saucepan of hot (not boiling) water, melt together chocolate, butter and espresso powder, stirring occasionally. Spread 1 tsp (5 mL) onto bottom of cookie; sandwich with bottom of second cookie. Dip both ends into chocolate mixture. Let stand on rack until set. Repeat with remaining cookies and chocolate mixture. Makes about 24 cookies.

Cinnamon Stars

2-1/2 cups	hazelnuts (unskinned) or walnuts	625 mL
3	egg whites	3
Pinch	each salt and cream of tartar	Pinch
1-1/2 cups	granulated sugar	375 mL
2 tsp	cinnamon	10 mL
1/2 tsp	vanilla	2 mL

● In food processor, pulse nuts until coarsely ground; transfer to large bowl. In separate bowl, beat egg whites until frothy; beat in salt and cream of tartar. Beat in 1 cup (250 mL) of the sugar, 2 tbsp (25 mL) at a time, until stiff glossy peaks form, about 5 minutes. Beat in cinnamon and vanilla.

● Remove 1/2 cup (125 mL) of the meringue; cover and refrigerate for topping. Stir remaining meringue into ground nuts to form dense sticky dough; cover and refrigerate for at least 2 hours or for up to 6 hours.

● Sprinkle work surface generously with some of the remaining sugar. Working with one-third of the dough at a time, place on work surface and sprinkle with some of the sugar. Dampen rolling pin with moist towel.

● Roll out dough to scant 1/4-inch (5 mm) thickness, remoistening pin whenever lifted. Using 2-inch (5 cm) star-shaped cookie cutter, cut out shapes; place on parchment or waxed paper-lined baking sheets.

● With small palette knife or brush, gently spread 2 tsp (10 mL) reserved meringue over each cookie. Bake in 300°F (150°C) oven for about 30 minutes or until crisp. Makes about 48 cookies.

These crisp star-shaped cookies are a tradition during the German festive season. Although they take a little more effort to make than regular festive treats, the delicious results are more than worth it.

Per cookie: about
- 70 calories
- 1 g protein
- 4 g fat
- 7 g carbohydrate

TIP: Be sure to keep remoistening your rolling pin as you work to prevent the dough from sticking.

Chocolate Kisses

4	egg whites	4
1/4 tsp	cream of tartar	1 mL
1 cup	granulated sugar	250 mL
2 tbsp	unsweetened cocoa powder	25 mL
3 oz	semisweet chocolate, coarsely chopped	90 g

● In large bowl, beat egg whites with cream of tartar until soft peaks form; gradually beat in sugar, 2 tbsp (25 mL) at a time, until stiff glossy peaks form.

● Using pastry bag or spoon, pipe meringue into 1-1/2-inch (4 cm) mounds on parchment paper-lined or greased and floured baking sheets. Sift cocoa over top. Bake in 200°F (100°C) oven for 2 hours or until dry. Turn off oven; let stand in oven for 1 hour or until cool.

● In bowl over saucepan of hot (not boiling) water, melt chocolate, stirring occasionally. Spread over bottom of 1 meringue; sandwich with bottom of second meringue. Repeat with remaining meringues. Makes about 36 cookies.

Chocolate is the divine glue holding together two dainty meringue kisses. Pretty and delicious, these little kisses suit showers, wedding sweet tables and open-house celebrations.

Per cookie: about
- 36 calories
- 1 g protein
- 1 g fat
- 7 g carbohydrate

Hamantaschen ◀

2/3 cup	butter, softened	150 mL
1 cup	granulated sugar	250 mL
3	eggs	3
3 tbsp	liquid honey	50 mL
1 tsp	vanilla	5 mL
3 cups	all-purpose flour	750 mL
1 tsp	baking powder	5 mL
	FILLING	
2 cups	dried apricots	500 mL
1 cup	golden raisins	250 mL
1 cup	orange juice	250 mL
1/4 cup	water	50 mL
2 tbsp	granulated sugar	25 mL
1 tsp	grated orange rind	5 mL
1	egg, lightly beaten	1

● In large bowl, beat butter with sugar until fluffy; beat in eggs, one at a time. Beat in honey and vanilla. Stir flour with baking powder; stir into butter mixture in three additions. Press gently into ball; wrap in plastic wrap and refrigerate for at least 2 hours or for up to 3 days.

● FILLING: In small saucepan, bring apricots, raisins and orange juice to boil; reduce heat and simmer, stirring occasionally, for 10 minutes. Let cool. In food processor, purée together cooled apricot mixture, water, sugar and orange rind until finely chopped.

● Divide dough into quarters. On lightly floured surface, roll out each portion to 1/8-inch (3 mm) thickness. Using floured 2-1/2-inch (6 cm) round cookie cutter, cut out shapes. Place heaping teaspoonful (5 mL) filling in center of each. Fold up three sides to make three corners; pinch each corner to seal.

● Place on greased baking sheets; brush edges with egg. Bake in 350°F (180°C) oven for 15 to 20 minutes or until golden. Makes about 60 cookies.

VARIATION
● PRUNE FILLING: In food processor, finely chop together 2 cups (500 mL) pitted prunes, 1 cup (250 mL) raisins, 1/2 cup (125 mL) walnuts, 1 tsp (5 mL) grated lemon rind, 1/4 cup (50 mL) lemon juice and 2 tbsp (25 mL) granulated sugar.

Tricornered hat-shaped hamantaschen, filled with dried fruit, poppy seeds or jam, are a traditional treat during Purim, one of the liveliest of the Jewish holidays.

Per cookie: about
- 85 calories
- 2 g fat
- 1 g protein
- 15 g carbohydrate

BAKING SHEETS

Choosing the Best
● Rimless baking sheets are ideal for cookies since the lack of sides allows free movement of air over the cookies and results in even baking and browning.
● If you must use rimmed sheets, be sure to monitor cookies closely while they bake, since cookies closer to the rims will not bake as quickly as the ones in the center of the sheet.
● The best baking sheets are sturdy, heavy aluminum or metal ones that are light in color. Avoid using dark-colored baking sheets because they absorb too much heat and can cause over-browning.
● Don't use insulated baking sheets when making crisp cookies — they won't crisp! Use regular baking sheets, instead.

Before and After Baking
● For most drop, sliced, rolled or shaped cookies, line baking sheets with parchment paper. Cookies lift off parchment paper effortlessly, and clean-up is easy, too — wipe paper after use and reuse until paper becomes dark and brittle.
● Alternatively, brush baking sheets lightly with shortening.
● If you have only one or two baking sheets, let them cool thoroughly between batches. Hot baking sheets will melt cookie dough, resulting in changes to the texture and shape of cookies.

Date-Filled Pinwheels

In Finland, where these rolled and folded cookies originate, the filling is often made with poppy seeds. A citrus-accented date filling is equally delicious.

Per cookie: about
- 137 calories
- 6 g fat
- 2 g protein
- 19 g carbohydrate

1 cup	butter, softened	250 mL
2/3 cup	packed brown sugar	150 mL
1	egg	1
1/2 tsp	vanilla	2 mL
2-2/3 cups	all-purpose flour	650 mL
1/2 tsp	baking powder	2 mL
1/2 tsp	grated lemon rind	2 mL
Pinch	each ground nutmeg and salt	Pinch
2 tbsp	icing sugar	25 mL
	FILLING	
3/4 cup	dates, coarsely chopped	175 mL
1/4 cup	packed brown sugar	50 mL
1/4 tsp	grated lemon rind	1 mL
1-1/2 tsp	lemon juice	7 mL
Pinch	ground nutmeg	Pinch

● In large bowl, beat butter with sugar until fluffy; beat in egg and vanilla. In separate bowl, stir together flour, baking powder, lemon rind, nutmeg and salt; with wooden spoon, gradually stir into butter mixture.

● Divide dough in half; wrap in plastic wrap and refrigerate for 30 minutes.

● FILLING: Meanwhile, in saucepan, combine dates, sugar, 1/4 cup (50 mL) water, lemon rind, lemon juice and nutmeg; bring to boil. Reduce heat and simmer, stirring often, for 5 to 10 minutes or until thickened. Let cool.

● Between waxed paper, roll out each portion of dough to 1/8-inch (3 mm) thick square. Using decorative pastry wheel or sharp knife, cut into 2-1/2-inch (6 cm) squares. On each corner of each square, make 1-inch (2.5 cm) diagonal cut toward middle.

● Place scant teaspoonful (5 mL) filling in center of each square. Lifting up every other corner tip of dough, fold each over filling and press together gently.

● Place on greased baking sheet. Bake in 350°F (180°C) oven for 12 to 15 minutes or until golden brown. Transfer to racks; let cool. Just before serving, dust with icing sugar. Makes about 30 cookies.

TIP: A small metal spatula comes in handy when you're lifting corners of the cookie dough from the waxed paper.

Spritz Cookies

Here's the foundation for any shape a cookie press will deliver — bars, wreaths, rosettes, hearts and more. Decorate with silver dragées, chopped candied fruit or a dusting of icing sugar.

Per cookie: about
- 75 calories
- 5 g fat
- 1 g protein
- 7 g carbohydrate

1 cup	butter, softened	250 mL
1/2 cup	granulated sugar	125 mL
1	egg	1
1 tsp	vanilla	5 mL
2 cups	all-purpose flour	500 mL

● In large bowl, beat butter with sugar until fluffy; beat in egg and vanilla. Using wooden spoon, gradually stir in flour.

● Fill cookie press with batches of dough; press out desired shapes onto chilled ungreased baking sheets. Decorate, if desired. Bake in 350°F (180°C) oven for 10 to 12 minutes or until very lightly browned. Makes about 40 cookies.

Rugulahs ▼

1	pkg (250 g) cream cheese, softened	1
1 cup	butter, softened	250 mL
2 tbsp	granulated sugar	25 mL
2 cups	all-purpose flour	500 mL
	FILLING	
1 cup	toasted coarsely chopped pecans	250 mL
1/2 cup	golden raisins (optional)	125 mL
1/4 cup	granulated sugar	50 mL
1/4 cup	packed brown sugar	50 mL
3/4 tsp	cinnamon	4 mL
3/4 cup	apricot jam	175 mL
	TOPPING	
1	egg	1
2 tbsp	coarse or granulated sugar	25 mL

● In large bowl, beat cream cheese with butter until fluffy; beat in sugar. Using wooden spoon, gradually stir in flour. Form into ball; cut into quarters and shape into rounds.

● Wrap each in plastic wrap; refrigerate for at least 2 hours or for up to 24 hours. Let stand at room temperature for 15 minutes before rolling.

● FILLING: In small bowl, combine pecans, raisins (if using), granulated sugar, brown sugar and cinnamon. In separate bowl, stir jam with 1 tsp (5 mL) water until spreadable.

● On lightly floured surface, roll out one round of dough into 11-inch (28 cm) circle. Spread 3 tbsp (50 mL) of the jam evenly over top; sprinkle with one-quarter of the nut mixture. Cut into 12 pie-shape wedges.

● Starting from wide end, roll up each wedge to form crescent shape. Place, about 2 inches (5 cm) apart, on foil- or parchment paper-lined baking sheets; refrigerate for 30 minutes. Repeat with remaining dough and filling.

● TOPPING: Beat egg lightly; brush over chilled cookies. Sprinkle sugar over top.

● Bake in 350°F (180°C) oven for about 25 minutes or until golden brown. Makes about 48 cookies.

VARIATION

● CHOCOLATE RASPBERRY RUGULAHS: Substitute chocolate chips for the raisins and raspberry jam for the apricot jam.

A fancy cookie is a must on the entertaining circuit. And none is more suited to those pleasurable occasions than this traditional Jewish crescent.

Per cookie: about
- 115 calories
- 7 g fat
- 1 g protein
- 11 g carbohydrate

TIP: If the jam you're using contains any large chunks, chop them up into smaller pieces before using.

Rugulahs (left) and Pistachio Shortbread (p. 56)

Sicilian X Cookies

A tender dough is rolled around a filling that epitomizes the Italian penchant for combining everything good in a single treat. The roll is then cut into sections and each end is split and spread to form an "X."

Per cookie: about
- 130 calories
- 6 g fat
- 2 g protein
- 18 g carbohydrate

2-1/2 cups	all-purpose flour	625 mL
1/2 cup	granulated sugar	125 mL
1/2 tsp	each baking powder and salt	2 mL
3/4 cup	butter	175 mL
2	eggs	2
1 tsp	grated orange rind	5 mL
1 tsp	vanilla	5 mL
2 tbsp	icing sugar	25 mL
	FILLING	
1/2 cup	hazelnuts	125 mL
1-1/2 tsp	instant coffee granules	7 mL
8 oz	dried figs, chopped	250 g
1/3 cup	chocolate chips	75 mL
1/4 cup	raisins	50 mL
1/4 cup	apricot or plum jam	50 mL
1/4 tsp	each cinnamon and ground cloves	1 mL

● In food processor or bowl, combine flour, sugar, baking powder and salt. Add butter; pulse or cut in with pastry blender or two knives until in fine crumbs. Add eggs, orange rind and vanilla; blend until in ball.

● On lightly floured surface, divide into thirds; press each into rectangle about 1 inch (2.5 cm) thick. Wrap in plastic wrap; refrigerate for about 30 minutes or until chilled.

● FILLING: Meanwhile, spread hazelnuts on baking sheet; bake in 350°F (180°C) oven for 8 to 10 minutes or until fragrant. Transfer to tea towel; rub until most of the skins are removed. Let cool.

● Dissolve instant coffee in 3 tbsp (50 mL) water. In food processor or in bowl and using chef's knife, chop together hazelnuts, coffee, figs, chocolate chips, raisins, jam, cinnamon and cloves until in chunky paste. *(Dough and filling can be refrigerated in separate airtight containers for up to 2 days.)*

● Between waxed paper, roll out each portion of dough to 12- x 9-inch (30 x 23 cm) rectangle. Cut lengthwise into three 3-inch (8 cm) wide strips.

● Spread 1/4 cup (50 mL) of the filling lengthwise along center of each strip. Brush sides with water; fold one side over filling and continue to roll log over to enclose filling and place seam underneath. Pat to flatten slightly and seal seam.

● Cut each log into four 3-inch (8 cm) long pieces. Make lengthwise cut, about 1-1/4 inches (3 cm) long, in both ends of each piece. Bend ends outward slightly to form X shape. With spatula, transfer to greased baking sheets.

● Bake in 375°F (190°C) oven for 15 to 20 minutes or until golden. Transfer to rack and let cool. Dust with icing sugar. Makes 36 cookies.

VARIATION

● MINI SICILIAN X COOKIES: These delicate cookies require careful handling. Roll out each portion of dough to 12- x 8-inch (30 x 20 cm) rectangle; cut lengthwise into four 2-inch (5 cm) wide strips. Fill each with 2 tbsp (25 mL) filling. Roll up as directed; cut each roll into six 2-inch (5 cm) long pieces. Shape and bake for 15 minutes.

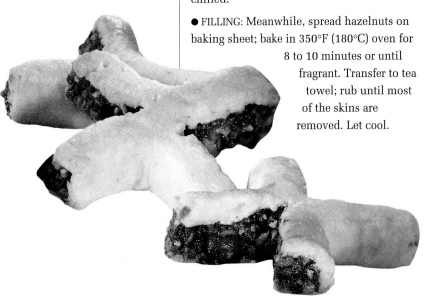

Vanilla Wreaths

1 cup	butter, softened	250 mL
1/2 cup	granulated sugar	125 mL
1/2 cup	marzipan (see box below)	125 mL
1 tbsp	vanilla	15 mL
1	egg	1
2 cups	all-purpose flour	500 mL

● In large bowl, beat butter with sugar until fluffy; beat in marzipan, vanilla and egg until smooth. Gradually beat in flour until consistency of whipped cream.

● Using large pastry bag fitted with medium rosette tip, pipe into 1-1/2-inch (4 cm) wreaths on greased baking sheets. Chill in refrigerator for 10 minutes.

● Bake in 375°F (190°C) oven for 10 to 12 minutes or until golden brown around edges. Makes about 84 cookies.

Make these delicate cookie wreaths, called vanillekranse *in Danish, for nibbling or for decorating and stringing on the tree (photo, p. 27). You can substitute commercial marzipan for the homemade.*

Per cookie: about
- 44 calories
- 1 g protein
- 3 g fat
- 4 g carbohydrate

MARZIPAN

● In bowl, cover 2 cups (500 mL) unblanched almonds (12 oz/375 g) with boiling water; let stand for 2 minutes. Drain and skin by firmly pressing one end to pop nut through skin.

● In food processor, grind warm almonds for 1-1/2 to 2 minutes or until fine. Add 2 cups (500 mL) icing sugar; mix for 1 minute or until blended. Blend in 2 tsp (10 mL) each almond extract and corn syrup.

● With motor running, pour in enough of 1 lightly beaten egg white to form ball. Wrap in plastic wrap and place in plastic bag; refrigerate for at least 2 hours or until firm. *(Marzipan can be refrigerated for up to 2 weeks or frozen for longer storage.)* Makes 1 lb (500 g) or 2 cups (500 mL).

Per tbsp (15 mL): about
- 83 calories • 2 g protein • 5 g fat • 9 g carbohydrate

Meringue Wreaths

2	egg whites	2
1 tsp	lemon juice	5 mL
1/4 tsp	cream of tartar	1 mL
2/3 cup	instant dissolving (fruit/berry) sugar	150 mL

● In bowl, beat egg whites with lemon juice until foamy. Add cream of tartar. Gradually beat in sugar, about 1 tbsp (15 mL) at a time, until stiff shiny peaks form. (A small amount rubbed between fingers should not feel gritty — sugar should be dissolved.)

● Using pastry bag fitted with star tip, pipe meringue into 1-1/2-inch (4 cm) rings on parchment paper- or foil-lined baking sheets. Bake in 250°F (120°C) oven for 1-1/4 hours or until firm. Turn off oven; leave meringues in oven for 1 hour. Makes 24 cookies.

Fancy cookies don't always suit guests with special diets, but these festive meringue wreaths are excellent for people following a gluten-free diet. While not low in calories because of the sugar, each cookie is small and has virtually no fat.

Per cookie: about
- 23 calories
- trace protein
- 0 g fat
- 6 g carbohydrate

Shortbread and Biscotti

Two of Canada's most popular cookies merit a chapter for themselves. Shortbread and biscotti both started out as simple treats — but today's creative bakers have transformed them into indulgences bursting with every favorite flavor.

Almond Shortbread Wedges ▶

From author, cooking teacher and television personality Bonnie Stern comes shortbread in a traditional wedge shape but with an exotic almond taste. Be sure to use almond paste as called for; do not use marzipan.

Per cookie: about
• 165 calories   • 2 g protein
• 10 g fat   • 16 g carbohydrate

1 cup	unsalted butter, softened	250 mL
8 oz	almond paste	250 g
1 cup	icing sugar, sifted	250 mL
Dash	almond extract (optional)	Dash
2 cups	all-purpose flour	500 mL

● Cut butter and almond paste into small pieces; place in large bowl or food processor. Add sugar; beat until well blended. Blend in almond extract (if using). Stir in flour until well blended.

● Pat dough into two 8-inch (20 cm) ungreased tart pans with removable bottoms, pressing into sides for fluted effect. With fork, press dough around edge to form pattern; prick center all over.

● Bake in 300°F (150°C) oven for 40 to 45 minutes or until very lightly browned. Remove sides of pans; gently cut each round into 12 wedges. Let cool on base on rack. Makes 24 cookies.

Brown Sugar Shortbread

These sugared rounds from Bonnie Stern offer all the rich, buttery flavor of traditional shortbread.

Per cookie: about
• 70 calories   • 1 g protein
• 4 g fat   • 3 g carbohydrate

1 cup	butter, softened	250 mL
3/4 cup	packed brown sugar, sieved	175 mL
2 cups	all-purpose flour	500 mL

● In large bowl, beat butter with brown sugar until very smooth and fluffy; stir in flour. Refrigerate for 1 hour.

● Shape into 1-inch (2.5 cm) balls. Place, 2 inches (5 cm) apart, on parchment paper-lined or greased and floured baking sheets. With bottom of glass or fork dipped in flour or sugar, or with floured cookie press, flatten balls. Bake in 300°F (150°C) oven for 20 to 30 minutes or until lightly browned. Makes 48 cookies.

TIP: To make crisp cookies, press them to 1/4-inch (5 mm) thickness.

Pistachio Shortbread ▼

*F*resh green pistachios add a
Middle Eastern note to the
butter, sugar and flour trio.

Per cookie: about
• 110 calories   • 2 g protein
• 8 g fat   • 9 g carbohydrate

3/4 cup	shelled pistachios	175 mL
1/2 cup	icing sugar	125 mL
1 cup	butter, softened	250 mL
1 tsp	vanilla	5 mL
2 cups	all-purpose flour	500 mL

● Place pistachios in tea towel; rub off excess skins. In food processor, combine 1/2 cup (125 mL) of the pistachios with 1/4 cup (50 mL) of the sugar; chop finely. Set aside. Coarsely chop remaining pistachios; set aside.

● In large bowl, beat butter with remaining sugar until light and fluffy; beat in vanilla. Gradually stir in flour and chopped pistachio-sugar mixture. Form into ball; divide in half and shape into rounds.

● Between sheets of waxed paper, roll out each round to 1/4-inch (5 mm) thickness. Using 2-inch (5 cm) crinkle-edge cookie cutter, cut out rounds, rerolling scraps once; place, 2 inches (5 cm) apart, on ungreased baking sheets.

● Sprinkle reserved pistachios in centers of cookies; press lightly into dough. Refrigerate for 15 minutes. Bake in 350°F (180°C) oven for about 12 minutes or just until starting to turn golden. Makes about 30 cookies.

TIP: Buy pistachios with partially opened shells. Closed shells mean that the delicately flavored nuts are immature. Avoid the red-dyed ones.

Peanutty Peanut Butter Shortbread

*P*eanut butter and shortbread
together in a square? Why
not? Satisfy lovers of both in
one pleasing bite.

Per cookie: about
• 150 calories   • 3 g protein
• 10 g fat   • 12 g carbohydrate

3/4 cup	unsalted butter, softened	175 mL
1/2 cup	crunchy peanut butter	125 mL
3/4 cup	icing sugar	175 mL
1	egg	1
1/2 tsp	vanilla	2 mL
2 cups	sifted cake-and-pastry flour	500 mL
1/2 tsp	baking powder	2 mL
Pinch	salt	Pinch
1/2 cup	salted peanuts, coarsely chopped	125 mL

● In large bowl, beat together butter, peanut butter and sugar; beat in egg and vanilla. In separate bowl, stir together flour, baking powder and salt; with wooden spoon, gradually stir into butter mixture.

● Spread in lightly greased 9-inch (2.5 L) square cake pan; press peanuts into dough. Bake in 350°F (180°C) oven for about 30 minutes or until firm in center and edges are golden brown. Let cool completely on rack before cutting into squares. Makes 24 cookies.

Espresso Shortbread

1 cup	unsalted butter, softened	250 mL
3/4 cup	granulated sugar	175 mL
2 cups	all-purpose flour	500 mL
1 tbsp	instant espresso powder	15 mL
1 tsp	finely grated lemon rind	5 mL

● In large bowl, beat butter with sugar until light and fluffy. In separate bowl, stir together flour, espresso powder and lemon rind; stir into butter mixture until combined. Pat into ungreased or parchment paper-lined 9-inch (2.5 L) square cake pan; prick all over with fork. Refrigerate for 1 hour.

● Bake in 300°F (150°C) oven for 45 to 50 minutes or until just light golden but not browned. Let cool in pan on rack before cutting into bars. Makes 30 cookies.

The unexpected addition of espresso with a twist of lemon is exquisite in these moist cake-like cookies from Bonnie Stern.

Per cookie: about
- 105 calories
- 1 g protein
- 6 g fat
- 11 g carbohydrate

Oatmeal Butterscotch Triangles

1 cup	butter, softened	250 mL
2/3 cup	packed brown sugar	150 mL
1/2 tsp	vanilla	2 mL
1-2/3 cups	all-purpose flour	400 mL
1 cup	rolled oats (not instant)	250 mL
3 oz	white chocolate, coarsely chopped	90 g
1/4 cup	red or green sugar	50 mL

● In large bowl, beat butter until fluffy; beat in brown sugar and vanilla until light. In separate bowl, stir flour with rolled oats; stir into butter mixture until blended. Cover and refrigerate for 30 minutes or until firm.

● On lightly floured surface, roll out dough to 1/4-inch (5 mm) thickness. Cut into four 6-inch (15 cm) circles, rerolling scraps as necessary. Place on greased baking sheets.

● Bake in 350°F (180°C) oven for about 15 minutes or until golden. Let cool on baking sheets for 10 minutes. Transfer to cutting board; cut each into 6 triangles.

● In bowl over saucepan of hot (not boiling) water, melt chocolate, stirring occasionally. Drizzle over triangles; sprinkle with colored sugar. Makes 24 cookies.

Drizzled white chocolate adds an unconventional but chic touch to shorties (photo, p. 14). The dough can also be shaped into balls and stamped with a cookie press.

Per cookie: about
- 163 calories
- 2 g protein
- 9 g fat
- 19 g carbohydrate

Ginger Shortbread

1 cup	butter, softened	250 mL
1/2 cup	icing sugar, sifted	125 mL
3 tbsp	finely chopped candied ginger	50 mL
1/4 tsp	salt	1 mL
2 cups	all-purpose flour	500 mL

● In large bowl, beat butter with sugar until fluffy; beat in ginger and salt. Gradually stir in flour.

● Between sheets of waxed paper, roll out dough to 1/4-inch (5 mm) thickness. Using floured 2-inch (5 cm) cookie cutter, cut out shapes; place, 2 inches (5 cm) apart, on ungreased baking sheets.

● Bake in 300°F (150°C) oven for 17 to 20 minutes or until light golden on edges. Makes about 65 cookies.

Susan Ross, first-prize winner in Canadian Living's cookie contest, cuts the shortbread into the shape of dog bones and gives them as gifts for Christmas.

Per cookie: about
- 44 calories
- trace protein
- 3 g fat
- 4 g carbohydrate

Chocolate Chunk Shortbread ▼

We guarantee you won't be able to have just one of these luscious chunky shortbread cookies. Just ask anyone who has sampled them at Desserts by Phipps, a popular north Toronto bakery and coffee shop.

Per cookie: about
- 100 calories
- 6 g fat
- 1 g protein
- 10 g carbohydrate

2-1/2 cups	all-purpose flour	625 mL
2 cups	butter, softened	500 mL
1 cup	instant dissolving (fruit/berry) sugar	250 mL
1 cup	sifted rice flour	250 mL
8 oz	milk chocolate, cut in chunks	250 g

● Spread 1-1/2 cups (375 mL) of the all-purpose flour on baking sheet; place under broiler 4 to 5 inches (10 to 12 cm) from heat. With oven door open, roast flour, turning with metal or wooden spatula every minute, for about 7 minutes or until medium brown color. Let cool to room temperature.

● In bowl, beat butter with sugar until light and fluffy. Sift together rice flour, roasted flour and remaining all-purpose flour; stir vigorously into butter mixture until well blended. Refrigerate for 1 hour. Stir in chocolate.

● Roll dough into 1-1/4-inch (3 cm) balls. Place, 2 inches (5 cm) apart, on ungreased baking sheets; flatten slightly. Bake in center of 275°F (140°C) oven for 50 minutes or until light golden. Makes about 72 cookies.

TIP: Fruit, or berry, sugar is more finely granulated than regular sugar and is sometimes called instant dissolving sugar, bar sugar or castor sugar. It is not icing sugar.

Simply the Best Shortbread

We've tasted a lot of delicious shortbread in the Test Kitchen but this superb extra-tender one from the Christmas bazaar at Vancouver's historic Hycroft House is still the best.

Per cookie: about
- 113 calories
- 8 g fat
- 1 g protein
- 10 g carbohydrate

1 cup	butter, softened	250 mL
3 tbsp	cornstarch	50 mL
1/4 cup	granulated sugar	50 mL
1-3/4 cups	all-purpose flour	425 mL

● In large bowl, beat butter until fluffy; gradually beat in cornstarch, then sugar. With wooden spoon, beat in flour, about 1/4 cup (50 mL) at a time.

● On lightly floured surface, roll out dough to 1/4-inch (5 mm) thickness. Using floured fluted 2-inch (5 cm) round cookie cutter, cut out cookies.

● Place on waxed paper-lined trays; prick each cookie three times with fork. Freeze until firm. (Cookies can be prepared to this point and stored in rigid airtight container in freezer for up to 1 month.)

● Place frozen rounds on ungreased baking sheet; bake in 275°F (140°C) oven for 40 to 50 minutes or until firm to the touch. Makes 24 cookies.

VARIATION
● LEMON POPPY SEED SHORTBREAD: Add 2 tbsp (25 mL) poppy seeds and 1 tbsp (15 mL) finely grated lemon rind to bowl before adding flour.

Candy Cane Shortbread ▲

2 cups	butter, softened	500 mL
1 cup	granulated sugar	250 mL
1/2 tsp	peppermint extract	2 mL
4 cups	all-purpose flour	1 L
1/3 cup	crushed candy canes	75 mL

● In large bowl, beat butter with sugar until fluffy; beat in peppermint extract. Stir in flour, 1/2 cup (125 mL) at a time, until combined. Divide into quarters; shape each into 4-inch (10 cm) long log.

● Wrap in plastic wrap and refrigerate for at least 2 hours or for up to 3 days. *(Dough can be frozen for up to 3 weeks.)*

● Using serrated knife, cut into 1/4-inch (5 mm) thick slices; place, 2 inches (5 cm) apart, on ungreased baking sheets. Bake in 350°F (180°C) oven for 10 minutes.

● Sprinkle 1/4 tsp (1 mL) crushed candy in center of each cookie; bake for 2 minutes or until firm to the touch, bottoms are golden and candies are melted. Makes about 60 cookies.

Looking for a bestseller for your bake sale? You've got it right here with these pretty pepperminty confections.

Per cookie: about
- 101 calories
- 6 g fat
- 1 g protein
- 11 g carbohydrate

Nutty Chocolate Espresso Biscotti ▼

These long and elegant cookies (biscotti means "baked twice" in Italian) are ideal dunked in a cup of morning coffee or in a glass of dessert wine later in the day.

Per cookie: about
- 202 calories
- 8 g fat
- 5 g protein
- 30 g carbohydrate

1-3/4 cups	all-purpose flour	425 mL
2/3 cup	unsweetened cocoa powder, sifted	150 mL
1 tbsp	espresso powder or instant coffee granules	15 mL
1 tsp	baking soda	5 mL
Pinch	salt	Pinch
3/4 cup	chopped unblanched almonds, toasted	175 mL
4 oz	semisweet chocolate, coarsely chopped	125 g

4	eggs	4
1 cup	granulated sugar	250 mL
1 tsp	vanilla	5 mL

● In large bowl, stir together flour, cocoa, espresso powder, baking soda and salt; stir in almonds and chocolate.

● In separate bowl, whisk 3 of the eggs until frothy; gradually whisk in sugar. Stir in vanilla. Make well in center of dry ingredients; pour in egg mixture, stirring with wooden spoon until stiff dough forms.

● Turn out dough onto lightly floured surface; shape into smooth 9- x 5-inch (23 x 12 cm) rectangle. Using spatulas, carefully transfer to greased baking sheet. Beat remaining egg; brush over dough. Bake in 350°F (180°C) oven for 30 minutes; let cool on pan on rack for 15 minutes.

● Transfer to cutting board. With serrated knife and starting at about 45-degree angle, cut into 1/2-inch (1 cm) thick slices. Stand slices up, slightly apart, on baking sheet; bake for 20 minutes longer or until firm. Makes 16 cookies.

Christmas Biscotti

1-1/3 cups	all-purpose flour	325 mL
1/2 tsp	baking soda	2 mL
1/2 tsp	aniseed, crushed	2 mL
1/4 cup	each red and green candied cherries, chopped	50 mL
2	eggs	2
1/3 cup	granulated sugar	75 mL
1 tsp	vanilla	5 mL
	TOPPING	
1	egg white, beaten	1
1 tsp	granulated sugar	5 mL

● In large bowl, stir together flour, baking soda and aniseed; stir in red and green cherries.

● In separate bowl, whisk together eggs, sugar and vanilla; stir into flour mixture to make soft sticky dough. Turn out onto lightly floured surface; divide in half and place on greased baking sheet. Shape into two 9- x 3-inch (23 x 8 cm) rectangles.

● TOPPING: Brush dough with egg white; sprinkle with sugar. Bake in 350°F (180°C) oven for 15 to 18 minutes or until light golden on top and golden brown on sides. Let cool on pan on rack for 10 minutes.

● Transfer to cutting board. With serrated knife, cut diagonally into 1/2-inch (1 cm) thick slices. Stand slices up, about 1/2 inch (1 cm) apart, on baking sheet; bake in 275°F (140°C) oven for 35 to 40 minutes or until golden and completely dry. Makes 24 cookies.

Home economist Emily Richards often bakes cookies that reflect her Italian heritage. Her biscotti include aniseed for its distinct sweet and authentic licorice flavor. You can replace candied cherries with 1/4 cup (50 mL) dried cherries and 1/4 cup (50 mL) shelled pistachio nuts.

Per cookie: about
- 57 calories
- 1 g fat
- 1 g protein
- 12 g carbohydrate

COOKIE-BAKING BASICS

Ingredients

● Butter is the best fat for flavor and appearance and should be softened to room temperature.

● Chop or dice candied or dried fruit with kitchen shears dipped in granulated sugar. A food processor often makes dried fruit gummy, but if you prefer to use one, combine fruit with some of the recipe's flour and use an on/off pulse motion just until chopped.

● Beat, butter, sugar, eggs and flavorings with an electric mixer. Use low speed or wooden spoon to stir in dry ingredients. For tender cookies, fold in the last of the flour and don't overbeat.

Dough

● When rolling out dough for cookies, work in as little extra flour from the surface and rolling pin as possible.

● Use a pastry cloth and stockinette-covered rolling pin, or roll out between two sheets of waxed paper.

● Roll out only part of the dough at a time, keeping the rest refrigerated.

● If using cutters, flour and cut out as many as possible in the first rolling, rerolling scraps only once for best results.

● Chilling cut-out cookies before baking them helps cookies keep their shape while baking and ensures tender results.

● Place unbaked cookies on cool baking sheets. Unless otherwise indicated, space about 2 inches (5 cm) apart to allow for spreading when baking; thin doughs spread more than thick.

Storage

● Let cookies firm up on baking sheet before lifting onto wire racks to cool.

● Let cookies cool to room temperature before storing.

● Store crisp and soft cookies in separate containers. Store crisp cookies between sheets of waxed paper in a loosely covered container. Store soft cookies in an airtight one so they stay moist and chewy.

Freezing

● You can freeze almost any cookie except meringues, or glazed or iced cookies unless specified in recipe.

● To package cookies for freezing, line airtight container with plastic wrap, then layer cookies in container between sheets of waxed paper. Place waxed paper on top so cookies avoid contact with ice crystals, then seal with tight-fitting lid.

● Most baked cookies can be frozen for up to 6 months.

● Most unbaked doughs can be frozen for up to 1 month. Label and date the package, including baking instructions.

Kmishbroit ◄

4	eggs	4
1 cup	granulated sugar	250 mL
1-1/2 cups	chopped almonds	375 mL
1 cup	vegetable oil	250 mL
3 cups	all-purpose flour	750 mL
1 tbsp	baking powder	15 mL
Pinch	salt	Pinch
	TOPPING	
3 tbsp	granulated sugar	50 mL
2 tbsp	cinnamon	25 mL

● In large bowl, beat eggs with sugar; stir in almonds and oil. In separate bowl, stir together flour, baking powder and salt; stir into egg mixture. Let stand for 30 minutes.

● Divide dough into thirds; shape each into 8-inch (20 cm) long log. Place on greased baking sheet; bake in 375°F (190°C) oven for 20 minutes. Let cool on pan on rack for 10 minutes. Transfer to cutting board. Cut into 3/4-inch (2 cm) thick slices; place, cut side down, on baking sheets.

● TOPPING: Stir sugar with cinnamon; sprinkle half over cookies. Bake in 325°F (160°C) oven for 15 minutes. Turn cookies over; sprinkle with remaining topping. Bake for 15 minutes longer or until golden. Makes about 24 cookies.

Toronto restaurant reviewer Cynthia Wine includes double-baked Jewish cookies by her mother, Ada Berney, in her Hanukkah party spread. This cookie is also known as Mandelbroit and is sometimes dipped into tea.

Per cookie: about
• 235 calories • 4 g protein
• 14 g fat • 24 g carbohydrate

Honey Nut Oat Biscotti

1/2 cup	butter, softened	125 mL
2/3 cup	packed brown sugar	150 mL
1/2 cup	liquid honey	125 mL
2	eggs	2
2 tsp	vanilla	10 mL
2-1/2 cups	all-purpose flour	625 mL
1 cup	quick-cooking rolled oats	250 mL
1 cup	chopped pecans, toasted	250 mL
2 tsp	cinnamon	10 mL
1 tsp	baking powder	5 mL
1/4 tsp	each baking soda and salt	1 mL

● In large bowl, beat butter with sugar until fluffy; beat in honey. Beat in eggs, one at a time; beat in vanilla. In separate bowl, stir together flour, rolled oats, pecans, cinnamon, baking powder, baking soda and salt; stir into butter mixture.

● Divide dough in half; place on greased baking sheet. Shape each into 10-inch (25 cm) long log. Bake in 350°F (180°C) oven for 30 minutes or until lightly browned. Let cool on pan for 5 minutes.

● Transfer to cutting board. With serrated knife, cut diagonally into 1/2-inch (1 cm) thick slices. Stand slices up, slightly apart, on baking sheet; bake in 325°F (160°C) oven for 25 to 30 minutes or until golden and almost firm to the touch. Makes 30 cookies.

VARIATION
● HONEY NUT APRICOT BISCOTTI: For this softer, less crunchy version of the classic biscotti, reduce pecans to 3/4 cup (175 mL) and add 1/2 cup (125 mL) chopped dried apricots.

These crunchy delights lean toward a tall glass of milk as accompaniment.

Per cookie: about
• 145 calories • 2 g protein
• 6 g fat • 20 g carbohydrate

Classic Biscotti ▶

One recipe, three great flavors — what more could any biscotti lover want?

Per cookie: about
• 115 calories
• 3 g protein
• 5 g fat
• 14 g carbohydrate

1-1/3 cups	all-purpose flour	425 mL
2 tsp	baking powder	10 mL
3/4 cup	whole unblanched almonds	175 mL
2	eggs	2
3/4 cup	granulated sugar	175 mL
1/3 cup	butter, melted	75 mL
2 tsp	vanilla	10 mL
1/2 tsp	almond extract	2 mL
1-1/2 tsp	grated orange rind	7 mL
1	egg white, lightly beaten	1

● In large bowl, stir together flour, baking powder and almonds. In separate bowl, whisk together eggs, sugar, butter, vanilla, almond extract and orange rind: stir into flour mixture to form soft sticky dough.

● Transfer to lightly floured surface; form into ball. Divide in half; roll each into 12-inch (30 cm) long log. Transfer to ungreased baking sheet.

● Brush tops with egg white; bake in 350°F (180°C) oven for 20 minutes. Let cool on pan on rack for 5 minutes.

● Transfer to cutting board; cut diagonally into 3/4-inch (2 cm) thick slices. Stand slices up, slightly apart, on baking sheet; bake for 20 to 25 minutes longer or until golden. Makes about 24 cookies.

VARIATIONS

● CHOCOLATE CHIP BISCOTTI: Add 1/2 cup (125 mL) chocolate chips to flour mixture.

● HAZELNUT BISCOTTI: Substitute 3/4 cup (175 mL) whole hazelnuts for almonds. Omit almond extract.

Cherry Almond Biscotti

Dried cherries (or other dried fruit such as raisins, cranberries, blueberries or slivered apricots) soften a traditionally hard dunking cookie. If replacing the almonds with another nut (such as pecans, pine nuts or hazelnuts), omit almond extract and increase vanilla to 1-1/2 tsp (7 mL).

Per cookie: about
• 98 calories
• 2 g protein
• 4 g fat
• 15 g carbohydrate

1/2 cup	butter, softened	125 mL
1 cup	granulated sugar	250 mL
3	eggs	3
1 tsp	each vanilla and almond extract	5 mL
2-3/4 cups	all-purpose flour	675 mL
1-1/2 tsp	baking powder	7 mL
1/4 tsp	salt	1 mL
3/4 cup	dried cherries	175 mL
1/2 cup	blanched almonds	125 mL
1 tbsp	icing sugar	15 mL

● In large bowl, beat butter with sugar until fluffy. Beat in eggs, one at a time; beat in vanilla and almond extract. In separate bowl, stir together flour, baking powder and salt; add to butter mixture all at once, stirring just until combined. Mix in cherries and almonds.

● Turn out dough onto lightly floured surface. Divide in half; shape each into 12-inch (30 cm) long log. Place, about 4 inches (10 cm) apart, on greased baking sheet; flatten until about 3 inches (8 cm) wide, leaving top slightly rounded.

● Bake in 325°F (160°C) oven for about 30 minutes or until firm and just beginning to turn golden on top. Let cool on pan on rack for 10 minutes.

● Transfer to cutting board. With serrated knife, cut diagonally into 1/2-inch (1 cm) thick slices. Stand slices up, slightly apart, on baking sheets; bake for 30 to 40 minutes or until dry and crisp. Let cool on rack. Dust with icing sugar. Makes about 40 cookies.

Squares, Bars and Friends

If you're a lover of bars and squares, we guarantee you won't be able to resist this collection of best-ever layers stacked with all your favorite fillings — from citrusy orange and sour cherry to super-rich cappuccino, maple walnut and tiramisu.

Hawaiian Bars ▶

Dried papaya, pineapple and macadamia nuts bespeak Hawaii, but you can use other dried fruit and nuts — apricots and almonds, for example — and these bars from associate food director Daphna Rabinovitch will be just as tasty.

Per bar: about
- 175 calories
- 8 g fat
- 2 g protein
- 26 g carbohydrate

1/2 cup	unsalted butter, softened	125 mL
3/4 cup	packed brown sugar	175 mL
2 tsp	white vinegar	10 mL
1 tsp	vanilla	5 mL
2 cups	all-purpose flour	500 mL
Pinch	salt	Pinch
	TOPPING	
3	eggs	3
3/4 cup	packed brown sugar	175 mL
1 tsp	vanilla	5 mL
2 cups	flaked coconut	500 mL
1 cup	each chopped dried pineapple and papaya	250 mL
1 cup	chopped lightly salted macadamia nuts	250 mL

● Lightly grease 13- x 9-inch (3.5 L) cake pan; line with foil, leaving 2-inch (5 cm) overhang on each long side. Set aside.

● In bowl, beat butter with sugar; beat in vinegar and vanilla. With wooden spoon, gradually stir in flour and salt to form crumbly dough. Gently press handfuls of dough together; press into prepared pan.

● Bake in 350°F (180°C) oven for 15 to 20 minutes or until lightly browned. Let cool on rack for 15 minutes.

● TOPPING: In bowl, beat together eggs, sugar and vanilla for about 2 minutes or until smooth; stir in coconut, pineapple, papaya and nuts. Pour over base, smoothing top; bake for 30 to 35 minutes or until lightly browned. Let cool completely on rack.

● With knife, cut along ends of pan; using foil overhang, loosen from pan. Invert onto back of baking sheet; peel off foil. Invert onto board; cut into bars. Makes 32 bars.

TIP: To make chopping easier, snip dried fruit into pieces with kitchen scissors.

(Clockwise from top) Cappuccino Nanaimo Bar (p. 75), two Hawaiian Bars, Lemon Walnut Square (p. 72)

Almond Apricot Squares ▲

A *sixties classic gets a light and trendy update from Toronto food writer Anne Lindsay.*

Per square: about
- 123 calories
- 5 g fat
- 2 g protein
- 18 g carbohydrate

3/4 cup	packed dried apricots	175 mL
1/4 cup	butter	50 mL
1 cup	all-purpose flour	250 mL
3/4 cup	granulated sugar	175 mL
2 tbsp	1% plain yogurt	25 mL
2	eggs	2
Pinch	salt	Pinch
1/2 cup	slivered almonds	125 mL

● In small saucepan or microwaveable dish, combine apricots with enough water to cover. Cover and bring to boil, or microwave at High for 1 minute. Remove from heat; let stand for 1 minute. Drain and let cool; chop finely and set aside.

● In bowl and using pastry blender or two knives, cut butter into flour until in fine crumbs. Stir in 1/4 cup (50 mL) of the sugar and yogurt until combined. Press into greased 8-inch (2 L) square cake pan; bake in 350°F (180°C) oven for about 20 minutes or until golden.

● Meanwhile, in bowl, beat together eggs, remaining sugar and salt just until combined; stir in apricots. Pour over base; sprinkle with almonds. Bake in 350°F (180°C) oven for about 30 minutes or until set and golden brown. Let cool on rack; cut into squares. Makes 18 squares.

Lemon Almond Bars

3/4 cup	butter, softened	175 mL
1/2 cup	granulated sugar	125 mL
1/4 tsp	salt	1 mL
2 cups	all-purpose flour	500 mL
	TOPPING	
4	eggs	4
1-1/2 cups	granulated sugar	375 mL
1/4 cup	all-purpose flour	50 mL
2 tbsp	grated lemon rind	25 mL
1/3 cup	lemon juice	75 mL
1-1/2 cups	sliced almonds	375 mL

● In bowl, beat together butter, sugar and salt until light; stir in flour. Press into ungreased 13- x 9-inch (3.5 L) cake pan; bake in 325°F (160°C) oven for about 35 minutes or until golden.

● TOPPING: In bowl, whisk together eggs, sugar, flour, lemon rind and juice until smooth; pour over base. Sprinkle with almonds; bake for 20 to 25 minutes or until set. Let cool on rack; cut into bars. Makes 30 bars.

A buttery base, tangy topping and sprinkle of toasted nuts add up to a lovely treat that suits both casual and elegant occasions.

Per bar: about
- 168 calories
- 8 g fat
- 3 g protein
- 22 g carbohydrate

Linzer Bars

2-1/3 cups	hazelnuts	575 mL
1 cup	granulated sugar	250 mL
2 cups	all-purpose flour	500 mL
2 tbsp	unsweetened cocoa powder	25 mL
1/2 tsp	cinnamon	2 mL
Pinch	ground cloves	Pinch
1 cup	butter, cubed	250 mL
2	eggs	2
2 cups	apricot jam	500 mL

● Spread hazelnuts on baking sheet; bake in 350°F (180°C) oven for 8 to 10 minutes or until fragrant and skins begin to crack. Transfer to tea towel. Rub until most of the skins are removed.

● In food processor, chop hazelnuts and 3/4 cup (175 mL) of the sugar until fine. Add remaining sugar, flour, cocoa, cinnamon and cloves; pulse to mix. Add butter; pulse until mixture resembles oatmeal. With machine running, add eggs, processing just until dough forms ball.

● Divide dough in half; wrap in plastic wrap and refrigerate for 15 minutes. Between waxed paper, roll out one of the portions to 15- x 10-inch (38 x 25 cm) rectangle. Slide paper and dough onto baking sheet; refrigerate until firm, at least 1 hour.

● Between waxed paper, roll out remaining dough to same-size rectangle; slide onto flat pan. Remove top sheet of paper; invert onto foil-lined 15- x 10-inch (40 x 25 cm) jelly roll pan. Peel off paper; press dough to fit base and up sides of pan. Spread apricot jam evenly over dough.

● Cut chilled dough lengthwise into 1/2-inch (1 cm) wide strips. Starting at top right corner of pan, lay 1 of the strips diagonally to opposite corner over jam. Lay parallel strips about 1 inch (2.5 cm) apart, cutting and patching strips to fit. Repeat in opposite direction to form diamond pattern.

● Bake in 375°F (190°C) oven for 40 to 45 minutes or until filling is bubbly and crust begins to darken slightly. Let cool on rack; cut into bars. Makes 40 bars.

Austria's famous linzertorte — with its buttery base and lattice-strip top that encloses a jam filling — is the inspiration for these delights.

Per bar: about
- 190 calories
- 11 g fat
- 2 g protein
- 22 g carbohydrate

Apple Raspberry Crumble Bars

Here's a lighter version of an old-fashioned layered bar that features fresh-tasting apples and raspberries.

Per bar: about
- 115 calories
- 1 g protein
- 4 g fat
- 18 g carbohydrate

2 cups	all-purpose flour	500 mL
3/4 tsp	salt	4 mL
1/3 cup	butter, cubed	75 mL
1/4 cup	canola oil	50 mL
1/3 cup	cold water	75 mL
4 tsp	lemon juice	20 mL
	FILLING	
5 cups	thinly sliced peeled apples (preferably Northern Spy)	1.25 L
1	pkg (300 g) individually frozen unsweetened raspberries	1
1 tbsp	lemon juice	15 mL
2/3 cup	granulated sugar	150 mL
3 tbsp	all-purpose flour	50 mL
1/2 tsp	cinnamon	2 mL
	CRUMBLE	
3/4 cup	rolled oats (not instant)	175 mL
3/4 cup	all-purpose flour	175 mL
3/4 cup	packed brown sugar	175 mL
1 tsp	cinnamon	5 mL
2 tbsp	butter, softened	25 mL
2 tbsp	cranberry or apple juice	25 mL
1 tbsp	canola oil	15 mL

● In food processor, combine flour with salt. Add butter and oil; pulse until in coarse crumbs. Combine water and lemon juice; gradually add to food processor, pulsing several times until mixture starts to hold together.

● Press evenly into 13- x 9-inch (3.5 L) cake pan; bake in 350°F (180°C) oven for 10 to 15 minutes or until lightly browned.

● FILLING: In bowl, toss together apples, raspberries and lemon juice. Add sugar, flour and cinnamon, stirring to coat fruit; spoon over base.

● CRUMBLE: In bowl, mix together rolled oats, flour, sugar and cinnamon; stir in butter, juice and oil until crumbly. Sprinkle over fruit.

● Bake in 400°F (200°C) oven for 10 minutes. Reduce heat to 350°F (180°C); bake for 30 to 35 minutes or until topping is browned and apples are tender. Let cool on rack; cut into bars. Makes 40 bars.

Pecan Butter Tart Squares

Arlene Bennett of Cape Breton, Nova Scotia, captures all the rich, sweet, buttery taste of ever-popular butter tarts in quick-to-make squares.

Per square: about
- 199 calories
- 2 g protein
- 11 g fat
- 25 g carbohydrate

2 cups	all-purpose flour	500 mL
2 tbsp	granulated sugar	25 mL
1 cup	butter, cubed	250 mL
	TOPPING	
3	eggs	3
2-1/4 cups	packed brown sugar	550 mL
3/4 cup	butter, melted	175 mL
1 tbsp	vinegar	15 mL
1-1/2 tsp	vanilla	7 mL
1-1/2 cups	currants or raisins	375 mL
1/2 cup	chopped pecans	125 mL
2 tbsp	icing sugar	25 mL

● In bowl, stir flour with sugar; using pastry blender or two knives, cut in butter until crumbly. Press into 13- x 9-inch (3.5 L) cake pan. Bake in 350°F (180°C) oven for 20 to 25 minutes or until set.

● TOPPING: In bowl, whisk eggs with sugar; whisk in butter, vinegar and vanilla. Stir in currants and pecans. Pour over base; bake for 30 to 40 minutes or until golden brown and slightly firm when touched, shielding edges with foil, if necessary, to prevent overbrowning. Let cool on rack. Cover and let stand at room temperature overnight; cut into squares. Sift icing sugar over top. Makes 35 squares.

Cranberry Crumble Squares

3/4 cup	butter, softened	175 mL
1/2 cup	granulated sugar	125 mL
1/2 tsp	vanilla	2 mL
1-1/2 cups	all-purpose flour	375 mL
1/2 cup	ground almonds	125 mL
1/2 tsp	cinnamon	2 mL
	FILLING	
2-1/2 cups	whole-berry cranberry sauce	625 mL
2 tsp	grated orange rind	10 mL
	TOPPING	
1/4 cup	all-purpose flour	50 mL
2 tbsp	packed brown sugar	25 mL
1/4 tsp	cinnamon	1 mL
2 tbsp	butter	25 mL
1/2 cup	chopped almonds	125 mL

● In bowl, beat together butter, sugar and vanilla until fluffy. Stir in flour, almonds and cinnamon to form loose crumbly dough. Pat into 13- x 9-inch (3 L) baking dish; bake in 375°F (190°C) oven for 25 minutes or until set and golden. Let cool slightly.

● TOPPING: In bowl, stir together flour, sugar and cinnamon; with pastry blender or two knives, cut in butter until crumbly. Stir in nuts. Set aside.

● FILLING: Stir cranberry sauce with orange rind; spread over base.

● Sprinkle evenly with topping. Bake for about 25 minutes or until topping is golden. Let cool completely; cut into squares. Makes 32 squares.

Cranberries add lush color to a comfy confection. These attractive squares (photo, p. 30) make a pleasing addition to a potluck supper. For a satisfying dessert, cut into generous pieces and serve with vanilla ice cream.

Per square: about
- 138 calories
- 7 g fat
- 2 g protein
- 18 g carbohydrate

Fruit, Nut and Coconut Bars

1-1/4 cups	all-purpose flour	300 mL
1/2 cup	granulated sugar	125 mL
1/2 cup	butter	125 mL
1	egg yolk	1
	TOPPING	
1	can (300 mL) sweetened condensed milk	1
2 tbsp	all-purpose flour	25 mL
2 tbsp	brandy or rye whisky	25 mL
3/4 cup	shredded coconut	175 mL
1/2 cup	chopped toasted walnuts	125 mL
1/2 cup	toasted slivered almonds	125 mL
1/2 cup	candied peel	125 mL
1/2 cup	chopped glacé cherries	125 mL

● In bowl, stir flour with sugar; using pastry blender or two knives, cut in butter until in fine crumbs. With fork, stir in egg yolk just until combined. Knead to form dough. Press evenly into greased 13- x 9-inch (3.5 L) cake pan. Bake in 350°F (180°C) oven for about 20 minutes or until golden.

● TOPPING: Meanwhile, in bowl, stir together condensed milk, flour and brandy; stir in coconut, walnuts, almonds, candied peel and glacé cherries until combined. Pour over base.

● Bake for 45 minutes or until golden and set. Let cool completely on rack; cut into bars. Makes 48 bars.

Here's the ultra-sweet, ultra-rich bar that makes a tray of dainties the center of attention. Cut them small and enjoy.

Per bar: about
- 99 calories
- 5 g fat
- 2 g protein
- 13 g carbohydrate

Lemon Walnut Squares

Fancy up the presentation of Daphna Rabinovitch's nutty-based citrus treats by cutting them small and serving them in tiny paper cups, just like truffles. These are excellent on bridal sweet tables (photo, p. 67).

Per square: about
- 125 calories
- 2 g protein
- 7 g fat
- 15 g carbohydrate

1 cup	all-purpose flour	250 mL
1/4 cup	icing sugar	50 mL
Pinch	salt	Pinch
1/2 cup	unsalted butter	125 mL
1/3 cup	finely chopped walnuts	75 mL
	TOPPING	
2	eggs	2
3/4 cup	granulated sugar	175 mL
1 tbsp	finely grated lemon rind	15 mL
1/4 cup	lemon juice	50 mL
2 tbsp	all-purpose flour	25 mL
1/2 tsp	baking powder	2 mL
1 tsp	icing sugar	5 mL

● In food processor or bowl, mix together flour, icing sugar and salt. Add butter; pulse or cut in with pastry blender or two knives until in fine crumbs. Stir in walnuts.

● Gently press handfuls of dough together; pat into greased 8-inch (2 L) square cake pan. Bake in 350°F (180°C) oven for 20 to 25 minutes or until golden. Let cool slightly on rack.

● TOPPING: Meanwhile, in bowl, beat eggs with sugar until pale and thickened; beat in lemon rind and juice, flour and baking powder. Pour over base.

● Bake for 25 to 30 minutes or until set in center and golden brown. Let cool completely on rack. Dust with icing sugar. Cut into squares. Makes 20 squares.

FOR THE BEST BARS AND SQUARES

1 Use pan size indicated. If pan is larger, bars will bake faster and become tough. If smaller, bars will be thicker with doughy centers.

2 Spread batter or base mixture evenly in pan for uniform thickness and texture.

3 For easy removal of bars and squares from pan, as well as a quick cleanup, line pan with foil, leaving enough overhang for "handles." When bars or squares are baked, lift out of pan using foil handles and transfer to cutting board.

4 When cutting bars, keep their richness and the occasion in mind — small for dinner parties, large for teenage gatherings.

5 Use ruler to mark off squares or bars evenly. Cut a cross through middle of pan first and work toward outside to keep cuts straight.

6 All bars and squares are best enjoyed fresh; however, if freezing, pack in rigid plastic wrap-lined container, layering between waxed paper. Place waxed paper on top so that no ice crystals come in contact with bars and squares, then seal with tight-fitting lid.

7 Thaw bars and squares for about 20 minutes at room temperature before serving.

(Clockwise from top) Glazed Apricot Blondies (p. 80), Crisp Peanut Slices (p. 88), Sour Cherry Almond Bars. (In corner) Mocha Hazelnut Nanaimo Bars (p. 76)

Sour Cherry Almond Bars ▲

1 cup	all-purpose flour	250 mL
1/2 cup	ground almonds	125 mL
1/3 cup	packed brown sugar	75 mL
1/3 cup	butter, cubed	75 mL
3/4 tsp	almond extract	4 mL
3/4 cup	sour cherry jam	175 mL
1 tbsp	lemon juice	15 mL
3/4 cup	sliced almonds	175 mL

● Grease 8-inch (2 L) square cake pan; line sides with waxed or parchment paper. Set aside.

● In food processor or bowl, mix together flour, ground almonds and sugar. Add butter; sprinkle with 1/4 tsp (1 mL) of the almond extract. Pulse or cut in with pastry blender or two knives until in coarse crumbs.

● Gently press handfuls of dough together; press evenly into prepared pan. Bake in 350°F (180°C) oven for about 15 minutes or until light golden; let cool on rack.

● In food processor or bowl, combine jam, remaining almond extract and lemon juice until smooth; spread evenly over base. Sprinkle with sliced almonds. Bake in 350°F (180°C) oven for 25 to 30 minutes or until bubbling and almonds are light golden. Let cool on rack; cut into bars. Makes 20 bars.

Y*ou can't beat the great taste combo of almonds and sour cherries, especially in these quick-to-make bars from food writer and author Rose Murray.*

Per bar: about
- 135 calories
- 7 g fat
- 2 g protein
- 18 g carbohydrate

TIP: You can double the quantity of these bars and bake in a 13- x 9-inch (3.5 L) cake pan for 5 minutes longer.

Margarita Bars

With lime, tequila and a splash of orange-flavored liqueur, this bar delivers the delicious taste of a margarita cocktail. No glass needed!

Per bar: about
- 120 calories
- 5 g fat
- 1 g protein
- 16 g carbohydrate

2 cups	all-purpose flour	500 mL
1/2 cup	granulated sugar	125 mL
1 cup	butter, cubed	250 mL
	TOPPING	
1-1/2 cups	granulated sugar	375 mL
2 tbsp	grated lime rind	25 mL
1/4 cup	all-purpose flour	50 mL
1 tsp	baking powder	5 mL
1/2 tsp	salt	2 mL
4	eggs	4
1/2 cup	lime juice	125 mL
2 tbsp	tequila liquor	25 mL
1 tbsp	Triple Sec liqueur	15 mL
2 tsp	icing sugar	10 mL

● In food processor or bowl, combine flour with sugar. Add butter; pulse or cut in with pastry blender or two knives until in coarse crumbs. Press into 13- x 9-inch (3.5 L) cake pan; bake in 350°F (180°C) oven for about 15 minutes or until golden brown. Let cool.

● TOPPING: In food processor, chop granulated sugar with lime rind until fine. Add flour, baking powder, salt and eggs; blend well. Combine lime juice, tequila and Triple Sec; add to flour mixture and mix just to combine. Pour over base.

● Bake in 350°F (180°C) oven for about 30 minutes or until set. Let cool on rack. Dust with icing sugar. Cut into bars. Makes 40 bars.

TIP: You can leave the bars uncut for storage in the refrigerator.

Tiramisu Nanaimo Bars

Two popular dessert indulgences come together in one irresistible bar. Since these bars are more softly set than most Nanaimos, serve on plates with forks.

Per bar: about
- 133 calories
- 9 g fat
- 1 g protein
- 12 g carbohydrate

1/3 cup	unsalted butter	75 mL
1/4 cup	sifted unsweetened cocoa powder	50 mL
2 tbsp	granulated sugar	25 mL
1 tbsp	Kahlua liqueur (optional)	15 mL
2 tsp	instant espresso powder	10 mL
1	egg, beaten	1
2 cups	vanilla wafer or ladyfinger crumbs (about 58 wafers)	500 mL
	TOPPING	
4 oz	mascarpone or cream cheese	125 g
1/3 cup	unsalted butter, softened	75 mL
1 tbsp	custard powder	15 mL
2 tsp	instant espresso powder	10 mL
1 cup	icing sugar	250 mL
3/4 oz	bittersweet chocolate, grated	20 g

● In small heavy saucepan, combine butter, cocoa, sugar, liqueur (if using) and espresso powder; cook over low heat, stirring, until melted and smooth. Stir in egg; cook, stirring constantly, until slightly thickened.

● Remove from heat; stir in crumbs. Press evenly into waxed paper-lined 8-inch (2 L) square cake pan. Refrigerate until cool.

● TOPPING: In bowl, beat mascarpone with butter until smooth; beat in custard powder and espresso powder. Gradually beat in icing sugar until smooth and light. Spread evenly over base; sprinkle with chocolate. Refrigerate until firm. Cut into small bars. Makes about 24 bars.

Cappuccino Nanaimo Bars

1/2 cup	unsalted butter	125 mL
1/3 cup	unsweetened cocoa powder	75 mL
1/4 cup	granulated sugar	50 mL
1	egg, lightly beaten	1
1-1/2 cups	graham cracker crumbs	375 mL
1 cup	shredded coconut	250 mL
1/2 cup	finely chopped walnuts	125 mL
	FILLING	
3 tbsp	unsalted butter	50 mL
2 tbsp	milk	25 mL
2 tsp	instant espresso powder or coffee granules	10 mL
1/2 tsp	vanilla	2 mL
2 cups	icing sugar	500 mL
	TOPPING	
4 oz	semisweet chocolate, coarsely chopped	125 g
1 tbsp	unsalted butter	15 mL
1/2 tsp	instant espresso powder	2 mL

● In heavy saucepan, heat together butter, cocoa, sugar and egg over low heat, stirring, until butter is melted. Remove from heat; stir in graham cracker crumbs, coconut and walnuts.

● Pat evenly into greased 9-inch (2.5 L) square cake pan. Bake in 350°F (180°C) oven for 10 to 12 minutes or until just firm. Let cool completely on rack.

● FILLING: In small saucepan, heat together butter, milk, espresso powder and vanilla over low heat until butter is melted and espresso powder dissolved. Transfer to bowl; let cool. Beat in sugar until thickened and smooth; spread over cooled base. Refrigerate for 45 minutes or until firm.

● TOPPING: Meanwhile, in bowl over saucepan of hot (not boiling) water, melt together chocolate, butter and espresso powder, stirring occasionally; spread over filling. With sharp knife, score topping only into bars. Refrigerate until topping is set. Cut into bars. Makes 24 bars.

This grown-up version of Nanaimo bars from associate food director Daphna Rabinovitch is a guaranteed bestseller at any bake sale (photo, p. 67).

Per bar: about
- 190 calories
- 12 g fat
- 2 g protein
- 22 g carbohydrate

Maple Walnut Bars

2 cups	all-purpose flour	500 mL
1/2 cup	granulated sugar	125 mL
1 cup	butter, cubed	250 mL
	TOPPING	
2 cups	walnut pieces or halves	500 mL
1 cup	packed brown sugar	250 mL
1/3 cup	butter	75 mL
3 tbsp	18% cream	50 mL
3 tbsp	corn syrup	50 mL
2 tbsp	maple syrup	25 mL
1/2 tsp	maple extract	2 mL

● In food processor or bowl, combine flour with sugar. Add butter; pulse or cut in with pastry blender or two knives until in coarse crumbs.

● Grease sides of 13- x 9-inch (3.5 L) cake pan; press flour mixture into pan. Bake in 350°F (180°C) oven for about 15 minutes or until golden. Let cool.

● TOPPING: Sprinkle walnuts over base. In heavy saucepan, combine brown sugar, butter, cream, corn syrup, maple syrup and maple extract; bring to boil over medium-high heat, stirring. Pour over nuts.

● Bake in 400°F (200°C) oven for 10 to 15 minutes or until bubbly. Let cool on rack; cut into bars. Makes 40 bars.

There's a double hit of crunchiness in these appealing bars — from tasty walnuts plus a crisp maple topping. Buy California walnuts whenever baking and, if possible, go the extra measure and get walnut halves rather than pieces. They are fresher and of higher quality.

Per bar: about
- 160 calories
- 10 g fat
- 2 g protein
- 16 g carbohydrate

Mocha Hazelnut Nanaimo Bars ▲

Once you've added the great flavor of coffee to a Nanaimo bar, you'll have one more reason to thank the folks in Nanaimo, B.C.

Per bar: about
- 154 calories
- 1 g protein
- 10 g fat
- 16 g carbohydrate

1-1/2 cups	graham cracker crumbs	375 mL
1 cup	flaked sweetened coconut	250 mL
1/2 cup	finely chopped toasted hazelnuts (see p. 12)	125 mL
2/3 cup	butter	150 mL
1/3 cup	unsweetened cocoa powder	75 mL
1/4 cup	granulated sugar	50 mL
1 tbsp	instant coffee granules	15 mL
1	egg, lightly beaten	1
	FILLING	
2 cups	icing sugar	500 mL
1/4 cup	butter, softened	50 mL
1 tbsp	instant coffee granules	15 mL
	MOCHA TOPPING	
2 tbsp	butter	25 mL
1 tbsp	instant coffee granules	15 mL
4 oz	semisweet chocolate, coarsely chopped	125 g

● In large bowl, stir together crumbs, coconut and hazelnuts; set aside.

● In saucepan, heat together butter, cocoa, sugar and coffee granules over low heat, stirring, until butter is melted. Remove from heat; whisk in egg. Stir into crumbs until well mixed. Press into greased 8-inch (2 L) square cake pan; bake in 350°F (180°C) oven for 10 minutes. Let cool on rack.

● FILLING: In bowl, beat half of the icing sugar with butter. Mix coffee granules with 2 tbsp (25 mL) water; beat into butter mixture along with remaining icing sugar. Spread over cooled base.

● MOCHA TOPPING: In bowl over saucepan of hot (not boiling) water, melt butter with coffee granules; add chocolate and stir until melted and smooth. Spread over filling.

● Refrigerate for about 2 hours or until chocolate is firm. Let stand at room temperature for 5 minutes to soften slightly before cutting into bars. Makes 32 bars.

Squamish Bars

1 cup	peanut butter	250 mL
1/2 cup	packed brown sugar	125 mL
1/2 cup	corn syrup	125 mL
1 cup	rice crisp cereal	250 mL
1 cup	corn flakes	250 mL
	FILLING	
2 cups	icing sugar	500 mL
1/4 cup	butter, softened	50 mL
2 tbsp	18% cream	25 mL
1-1/2 tsp	vanilla	7 mL
	TOPPING	
3 oz	bittersweet or semisweet chocolate, coarsely chopped	90 g
1 tbsp	butter	15 mL

● In large saucepan, heat together peanut butter, sugar and corn syrup over low heat until blended; remove from heat. Stir in rice crisp cereal and corn flakes; press into greased 9-inch (2.5 L) square cake pan; let cool.

● FILLING: In bowl, beat icing sugar with butter; beat in cream and vanilla. Spread over base; chill for 30 minutes.

● TOPPING: In bowl over saucepan of hot (not boiling) water, melt chocolate with butter, stirring occasionally; let cool. Spread over filling; chill for 20 minutes. Cut into bars. Makes 36 bars.

*F*irst Nanaimo, B.C., gave us a bar that became an instant hit — then Squamish, B.C., added peanut and crisp cereal, for a deliciously different take on a great Canadian classic.

Per bar: about
• 123 calories
• 2 g protein
• 6 g fat
• 16 g carbohydrate

Chocolate Almond Bars

1/4 cup	butter, softened	50 mL
2/3 cup	icing sugar	150 mL
1/2 tsp	vanilla	2 mL
1/2 cup	ground almonds	125 mL
1/4 cup	all-purpose flour	50 mL
Pinch	salt	Pinch
	TOPPING	
1/3 cup	butter	75 mL
1/2 cup	each packed brown sugar and corn syrup	125 mL
2 tsp	lemon juice	10 mL
3/4 cup	sliced almonds	175 mL
1/4 tsp	almond extract	1 mL
	GLAZE	
1 oz	semisweet chocolate, coarsely chopped	30 g

● In bowl, beat butter until creamy; gradually beat in sugar until light and fluffy. Beat in vanilla. Gradually stir in almonds, flour and salt. Pat evenly into greased 8-inch (2 L) square cake pan. Bake in 350°F (180°C) oven for about 12 minutes or until light colored.

● TOPPING: Meanwhile, in small saucepan, melt butter. Whisk in sugar, corn syrup, 1 tbsp (15 mL) water and lemon juice; bring to boil over medium-high heat, whisking. Boil, whisking, for 3 minutes or until thickened. Remove from heat. Stir in almonds and almond extract. Spread over base; bake for 15 minutes or until golden. Let cool slightly on rack.

● GLAZE: In bowl over saucepan of hot (not boiling) water, melt chocolate, stirring occasionally. With small spoon, drizzle over topping. Cut into bars. Let cool completely. Makes 16 bars.

A little candy, a little cookie — that's how to describe these decadent delights.

Per bar: about
• 196 calories
• 2 g protein
• 12 g fat
• 23 g carbohydrate

Brownies, Blondies and Co.

Brownies are the ultra-easy, ultra-pleasing square we all still love to make, and the ones we've included here are especially irresistible — along with blondie variations and effortless no-bake bars.

Caramel Pecan Brownies ▶

Adding caramel candies to an already-rich batter takes these brownies right over the top. Wow! Can't you just taste them?

Per brownie: about
- 236 calories
- 15 g fat
- 3 g protein
- 26 g carbohydrate

1	roll (52 g) soft caramel-and-milk-chocolate candy (such as Rolo)	1
4 oz	bittersweet or semisweet chocolate, coarsely chopped	125 g
2 oz	unsweetened chocolate, coarsely chopped	60 g
1/2 cup	butter, cubed	125 mL
1 cup	granulated sugar	250 mL
1 tsp	vanilla	5 mL
2	eggs	2
3/4 cup	all-purpose flour	175 mL
1/2 cup	chopped toasted pecans	125 mL
1/4 tsp	baking powder	1 mL
Pinch	salt	Pinch
2 tbsp	butterscotch sauce	25 mL

● Cut each caramel-chocolate candy piece into quarters; set aside.

● In heavy saucepan, melt together bittersweet and unsweetened chocolate and butter over low heat, stirring occasionally. Remove from heat; let cool slightly. Whisk in sugar and vanilla. Whisk in eggs, one at a time, until shiny.

● In bowl, stir together flour, half of the pecans, the baking powder and salt; stir gently into chocolate mixture just until combined.

● Spread in greased 8-inch (2 L) square cake pan. Drizzle with half of the butterscotch sauce. Scatter caramel-chocolate candy and remaining pecans over top; lightly press into batter without submerging. Drizzle with remaining sauce.

● Bake in 350°F (180°C) oven for 35 minutes or until cake tester inserted in center comes out clean. Let cool on rack. Cut into squares. Makes 16 brownies.

TIP: Caramilk candy bar (52 g) can be substituted for Rolo.

Caramel Pecan Brownies and Chocolate Chunk Shortbread (p. 58)

Classic Fudge Brownies

From the annual fair in Olds, Alberta, comes this prizewinning recipe for dense, moist saucepan brownies.

Per brownie: about
- 183 calories
- 3 g protein
- 12 g fat
- 19 g carbohydrate

1/2 cup	butter	125 mL
3 oz	unsweetened chocolate, coarsely chopped	90 g
1 cup	granulated sugar	250 mL
1 tsp	vanilla	5 mL
2	eggs, beaten	2
3/4 cup	all-purpose flour	175 mL
1/2 cup	chopped walnuts or pecans	125 mL

● In heavy saucepan, heat butter with chocolate over low heat until almost melted, stirring occasionally. Remove from heat; stir until completely melted. Stir in sugar, vanilla and eggs, blending well. Stir in flour and walnuts just until combined.

● Spread in greased 8-inch (2 L) square cake pan, smoothing top. Bake in 350°F (180°C) oven for 30 to 35 minutes or until cake tester inserted in center comes out clean. Let cool on rack; cut into squares. Makes 16 brownies.

Glazed Apricot Blondies

Blondies, the golden version of traditional brownies, suit any festive tray. You can double the recipe easily and bake in a 13- x 9-inch (3.5 L) pan, allowing an extra 10 to 15 minutes in the oven (photo, p. 73).

Per blondie: about
- 186 calories
- 2 g protein
- 8 g fat
- 27 g carbohydrate

1/2 cup	butter, softened	125 mL
1-1/4 cups	packed brown sugar	300 mL
2	eggs	2
2 tsp	vanilla	10 mL
1-1/4 cups	all-purpose flour	300 mL
1/4 tsp	salt	1 mL
1 cup	chopped dried apricots	250 mL
1/2 cup	chopped pecans	125 mL
	GLAZE	
1/2 cup	icing sugar	125 mL
2 tbsp	butter, softened	25 mL
2 tsp	lemon juice	10 mL

● In large bowl, beat butter with sugar until fluffy; beat in eggs, one at a time. Beat in vanilla. In separate bowl, stir together flour and salt. Stir in apricots and pecans; stir into butter mixture in two additions.

● Spread in greased 8-inch (2 L) square cake pan. Bake in 325°F (160°C) oven for 40 to 50 minutes or until cake tester inserted in center comes out clean. Let cool on rack until just slightly warm.

● GLAZE: In small bowl, stir together icing sugar, butter and lemon juice; spread over base. Let cool; cut into squares. Makes 20 blondies.

BROWNIE MINIATURES

Moist brownies baked in tiny paper cups make a delicious mouthful, especially when crowned by a chocolate Rosebud.

● In saucepan, heat together 1/3 cup (75 mL) packed brown sugar, 1/4 cup (50 mL) butter and 3 oz (90 g) coarsely chopped semisweet chocolate over low heat, stirring, until chocolate is just melted. Let cool for 1 minute. Blend in 1/2 tsp (2 mL) vanilla and 1 lightly beaten egg; gently fold in 1/3 cup (75 mL) all-purpose flour just until blended.

● Spoon into tiny paper baking cups. Bake in 350°F (180°C) oven for 10 to 12 minutes or until set. Remove from oven; set chocolate Rosebud on top of each (you will need 24). Let cool. Makes 24 brownie miniatures.

Per miniature: about • 60 calories • 1 g protein • 4 g fat • 7 g carbohydrate

TIP: Mint chocolate wafers, chocolate kisses or large chocolate chips can be substituted for the Rosebuds.

Crème de Menthe Brownies

1/2 cup	butter, softened	125 mL
1 cup	granulated sugar	250 mL
4	eggs	4
2 cups	chocolate syrup	500 mL
1 tsp	vanilla	5 mL
1 cup	all-purpose flour	250 mL
	ICING	
2 cups	icing sugar	500 mL
1/2 cup	butter, softened	125 mL
2 tbsp	crème de menthe liqueur	25 mL
	GLAZE	
1 cup	semisweet chocolate chips	250 mL
1/3 cup	butter	75 mL

● In large bowl, beat butter with sugar until fluffy. In separate bowl, whisk together eggs, chocolate syrup and vanilla; beat into butter mixture until blended. Fold in flour.

● Spread in greased 13- x 9-inch (3.5 L) cake pan. Bake in 350°F (180°C) oven for 30 to 35 minutes or until cake tester inserted in center comes out clean. Let cool on rack.

● ICING: In bowl, beat together sugar, butter and liqueur until smooth; spread over base. Refrigerate for 1 hour or until chilled.

● GLAZE: In small microwaveable bowl, microwave chocolate chips with butter at High for 1 to 1-1/2 minutes or until softened; stir until smooth. Spread over icing. Chill until firm, about 1 hour. Cut into squares. Makes 32 brownies.

*F*or St. Patrick's Day, try Teresa Craig's luscious brownies which first appeared in Canadian Living and the Blue Jays, a collection of recipes from the Toronto baseball team and their wives.

Per brownie: about
- 218 calories
- 2 g protein
- 11 g fat
- 31 g carbohydrate

Refrigerator Brownies

2-1/2 cups	graham cracker crumbs	625 mL
2 cups	miniature marshmallows	500 mL
1 cup	toasted chopped walnuts or pecans	250 mL
3/4 cup	icing sugar	175 mL
1 tbsp	grated orange rind	15 mL
2-1/2 cups	semisweet chocolate chips	625 mL
1 cup	evaporated milk	250 mL
2 tbsp	butter	25 mL
1 tsp	vanilla	5 mL

● In bowl, mix together graham cracker crumbs, marshmallows, walnuts, sugar and orange rind; set aside.

● In saucepan, heat together 2 cups (500 mL) of the chocolate chips, milk and butter over low heat until smooth, stirring occasionally. Remove from heat; stir in vanilla. Remove 1-1/4 cups (300 mL) chocolate mixture; stir into crumb mixture. Press into greased 8-inch (2 L) square cake pan.

● Add remaining chocolate chips to mixture in saucepan; whisk over low heat until melted. Spread over crumb mixture. Refrigerate for at least 1 hour or until firm. Cut into squares. Makes 18 brownies.

*N*o experience needed to make these no-bake chocolate bars! You can double the ingredients and use a 13- x 9-inch (3.5 L) pan.

Per brownie: about
- 287 calories
- 4 g protein
- 17 g fat
- 36 g carbohydrate

TIP: Be sure to use regular evaporated milk and not the lower-fat varieties for the brownies.

Megamocha Brownies ▲

These dense fudgy brownies, featured on the front cover, mellow deliciously when made ahead. For an attractive presentation (especially if packaging as gifts), cut cooled brownies on diagonal into diamond shapes. Dust half of each diamond with icing sugar, the other half with cocoa powder.

Per brownie: about
- 226 calories
- 14 g fat
- 3 g protein
- 26 g carbohydrate

1/2 cup	butter	125 mL
2 oz	unsweetened chocolate, coarsely chopped	60 g
1/2 cup	semisweet chocolate chips	125 mL
1 tbsp	instant espresso powder or instant coffee granules	15 mL
2	eggs	2
1 cup	granulated sugar	250 mL
1-1/2 tsp	vanilla	7 mL
Pinch	salt	Pinch
1/2 cup	all-purpose flour	125 mL
	GLAZE (OPTIONAL)	
1/2 cup	semisweet chocolate chips	125 mL
2 tbsp	18% cream or whipping cream	25 mL

● In bowl over saucepan of hot (not boiling) water, heat together butter, unsweetened chocolate, chocolate chips and espresso powder until nearly all chocolate is melted. Remove from heat; stir until smooth.

● In separate bowl, beat eggs with sugar until pale and thickened; stir in chocolate mixture, vanilla and salt. Fold in flour. Spread in greased 8-inch (2 L) square cake pan. Bake in 350°F (180°C) oven for 20 to 25 minutes or until edges pull slightly away from pan and cake tester inserted in center comes out with a few moist crumbs.

● GLAZE (if using): In bowl over saucepan of hot (not boiling) water, melt chocolate chips with cream, stirring until smooth. Spread over warm brownies. Let cool on rack; cut into squares. Makes 12 brownies.

White Chocolate Macadamia Brownies

6 oz	white chocolate, coarsely chopped	175 g
3/4 cup	granulated sugar	175 mL
2	eggs	2
1/3 cup	butter, melted	75 mL
2 tsp	vanilla	10 mL
1/2 tsp	finely grated orange rind	2 mL
1-1/4 cups	all-purpose flour	300 mL
3/4 tsp	baking powder	4 mL
Pinch	salt	Pinch
3/4 cup	coarsely chopped skinned macadamia nuts or hazelnuts, toasted (see p. 12)	175 mL
2 tsp	icing sugar	10 mL

● In bowl over saucepan of hot (not boiling) water, melt chocolate, stirring occasionally. In large bowl, whisk sugar with eggs until combined; slowly whisk in butter, vanilla and orange rind.

● In separate bowl, stir together flour, baking powder and salt; with wooden spoon, stir into butter mixture alternately with melted chocolate, making three additions of flour mixture and two of chocolate. Fold in nuts.

● Spread in greased 8-inch (2 L) square cake pan. Bake in 375°F (190°C) oven for about 30 minutes or until center is firm to the touch and cake tester inserted in center comes out with a few moist crumbs. Let cool on rack; cut into squares. Dust with icing sugar. Makes 25 brownies.

Add a creamy texture, nutty crunchiness and hint of orange, and the pleasure that brownies usually afford the palate rises a notch. Cut these brownies small and serve in tiny paper cups as you would chocolates or truffles.

Per brownie: about
- 141 calories
- 2 g protein
- 8 g fat
- 15 g carbohydrate

No-Bake Chocolate Ginger Bars

6 oz	semisweet chocolate, coarsely chopped	175 g
1/2 cup	butter, softened	125 mL
1/4 cup	granulated sugar	50 mL
1	egg	1
1-3/4 cups	coarsely crushed gingersnap cookies (8 oz/250 g)	425 mL
3 tbsp	chopped preserved ginger	50 mL
	ICING	
1	pkg (4 oz/125 g) cream cheese, softened	1
1/2 cup	icing sugar	125 mL
2 tbsp	unsweetened cocoa powder	25 mL

● In top of double boiler over simmering water, melt chocolate, stirring occasionally. Add butter and sugar; whisk until smooth. Whisk in egg; cook, whisking, for 3 minutes.

● Stir in cookie crumbs and ginger. Press into greased 8-inch (2 L) square cake pan. Cover and refrigerate for 30 minutes or until at room temperature.

● ICING: In food processor or bowl, beat cream cheese until fluffy; beat in icing sugar and cocoa until smooth. Spread over base. Refrigerate for at least 1 hour or until cold. Cut into bars. Makes 20 bars.

A smooth, not-too-sweet icing pairs nicely with a crunchy base that's studded with cookie crumbs and preserved ginger.

Per bar: about
- 185 calories
- 2 g protein
- 11 g fat
- 21 g carbohydrate

In box: Megamocha Brownies, Jam-Filled Sugar Cookies (p. 40). At left: Pistachio Shortbread (p. 56)

Fresh Plum Macaroon Squares ▶

Wonderful baker Iris Raven is the source of these fabulous — repeat, fabulous — cake-like squares topped with fresh plums nestled in an almond batter. Don't let a summer pass without making at least one batch.

Per square: about
- 225 calories
- 12 g fat
- 4 g protein
- 28 g carbohydrate

3/4 cup	butter, softened	175 mL
1 tbsp	grated orange rind	15 mL
3/4 cup	packed brown sugar	175 mL
1/2 cup	ground almonds	125 mL
1-1/2 cups	all-purpose flour	375 mL
	TOPPING	
1/4 cup	butter, softened	50 mL
1 cup	granulated sugar	250 mL
3/4 cup	all-purpose flour	175 mL
1/2 cup	sliced almonds	125 mL
3	eggs	3
1 tbsp	grated orange rind	15 mL
1/2 cup	ground almonds	125 mL
1/2 tsp	baking powder	2 mL
4 cups	sliced plums	1 L

● In bowl, beat butter with orange rind until creamy. Stir in sugar; stir in almonds. Gradually blend in flour, using fingertips when mixture becomes stiff.

● Grease sides of 13- x 9-inch (3.5 L) cake pan; press mixture into pan. Bake in 375°F (190°C) oven for 12 to 15 minutes or until lightly browned and firm to the touch.

● TOPPING: Meanwhile, in small bowl, combine butter and 1/4 cup (50 mL) each of the sugar and flour; mix in sliced almonds and set aside.

● In separate bowl, beat eggs with remaining sugar for about 5 minutes or until thickened and light; stir in orange rind. Combine remaining flour, ground almonds and baking powder; stir into egg mixture.

● Arrange plums evenly over base; spread egg mixture over top. Sprinkle with topping. Bake in 375°F (190°C) oven for 40 to 45 minutes or until top is puffed and golden and plums are tender when pierced with fork. Run knife around edge of pan; let cool on rack. Cut into squares. Makes 24 squares.

Honey Spice Fig Bars

One bite of these chewy bars and you'll wonder how anything so moist and tender could be made without any added fat such as butter. The secret is the applesauce.

Per bar: about
- 93 calories
- 1 g fat
- 1 g protein
- 21 g carbohydrate

1	egg	1
1 cup	liquid honey	250 mL
1/2 cup	unsweetened applesauce	125 mL
1 tsp	each grated lemon and orange rind	5 mL
1-3/4 cups	all-purpose flour	425 mL
1-1/2 tsp	cinnamon	7 mL
1 tsp	baking soda	5 mL
1/2 tsp	each ground ginger and allspice	2 mL
1-1/2 cups	finely chopped dried figs	375 mL
1/2 cup	slivered almonds	125 mL
	GLAZE	
1/2 cup	icing sugar	125 mL
4 tsp	lemon juice	20 mL

● In large bowl, whisk egg until frothy; whisk in honey, applesauce and lemon and orange rinds until smooth. In separate bowl, stir together flour, cinnamon, baking soda, ginger and allspice; stir into honey mixture. Stir in figs and almonds just until combined.

● Spread in greased 13- x 9-inch (3.5 L) cake pan. Bake in 350°F (180°C) oven for 22 to 25 minutes or until cake tester inserted in center comes out clean. Let cool on rack for 15 minutes.

● GLAZE: In small bowl, whisk icing sugar with lemon juice; brush over top. Let cool completely; cut into bars. Makes 36 bars.

Walnut Date Chews

2	eggs	2
1 cup	packed brown sugar	250 mL
1 cup	chopped dates	250 mL
1 tsp	vanilla	5 mL
1/2 cup	all-purpose flour	125 mL
1/4 tsp	each baking soda and salt	1 mL
1 cup	toasted chopped walnuts or pecans	250 mL
1 tsp	icing sugar	5 mL

● In large bowl, beat eggs with brown sugar until doubled in volume; stir in dates and vanilla. In separate bowl, stir together flour, baking soda and salt; stir into sugar mixture. Stir in nuts.

● Spread in greased 8-inch (2 L) square cake pan; bake in 350°F (180°C) oven for 20 to 30 minutes or until golden, crusty, edges are puffed and center underneath is still soft. Let cool on rack; cut into bars. Sift icing sugar over top. Makes 20 bars.

*R*ight in keeping with today's taste for lower-in-fat foods, this old favorite finds new appeal because it contains no butter.

Per bar: about
- 126 calories
- 2 g protein
- 4 g fat
- 21 g carbohydrate

TIP: To double the recipe for a 13- x 9-inch (3.5 L) pan, double ingredients and bake for 5 to 10 minutes longer than smaller pan, shielding edges with foil to prevent over-browning.

Applesauce Date Bars

Unsweetened applesauce puts zing into these comfy and casual treats.

Per bar: about
• 85 calories • 1 g protein
• 2 g fat • 15 g carbohydrate

1/4 cup	unsalted butter, softened	50 mL
1/2 cup	packed brown sugar	125 mL
1	egg	1
1 tsp	vanilla	5 mL
1-1/2 cups	all-purpose flour	375 mL
1 tsp	each cinnamon and unsweetened cocoa powder	5 mL
1/2 tsp	each baking powder and baking soda	2 mL
1/4 tsp	ground nutmeg	1 mL
Pinch	each ground cloves and salt	Pinch
3/4 cup	chopped dates	175 mL
1 cup	applesauce	250 mL
	TOPPING	
1/2 cup	icing sugar	125 mL
2 tsp	orange juice	10 mL

● In large bowl, beat butter with sugar; beat in egg and vanilla. In separate bowl, stir together flour, cinnamon, cocoa, baking powder, baking soda, nutmeg, cloves and salt; stir in dates. Fold into butter mixture alternately with applesauce, making three additions of flour mixture and two of applesauce.

● Spread in greased 8-inch (2 L) square cake pan; bake in 350°F (180°C) oven for 30 minutes or until cake tester inserted in center comes out clean. Let cool on rack.

● TOPPING: In small bowl, whisk icing sugar with orange juice; drizzle over cake. Cut into bars. Makes 24 bars.

TIP: An empty large salt shaker makes a great container for icing sugar to sprinkle over baked goods.

Apricot Granola Bars

Chock-full of moist coconut, crunchy peanuts and sweet dried apricots, these chewy granola bars are perfect for after-school or late-night snacking.

Per bar: about
• 135 calories • 3 g protein
• 7 g fat • 17 g carbohydrate

1/4 cup	unsalted butter	50 mL
1/4 cup	liquid honey	50 mL
1 tsp	vanilla	5 mL
1-1/2 cups	rolled oats (not quick-cooking)	375 mL
1/2 cup	slivered almonds	125 mL
1/2 cup	salted peanuts	125 mL
1/2 cup	flaked coconut	125 mL
3 tbsp	corn syrup	50 mL
1/2 cup	chopped dried apricots	125 mL
1/2 cup	raisins or chocolate chips	125 mL

● Lightly grease small baking sheet and 9-inch (2.5 L) square cake pan. Line cake pan with foil, leaving 2-inch (5 cm) overhang. Set both aside.

● In heavy saucepan, melt butter with honey over medium heat, stirring until smooth; remove from heat. Stir in vanilla; stir in rolled oats, almonds, peanuts and coconut until well coated. Quickly spread onto greased baking sheet; bake in 350°F (180°C) oven, stirring twice, for 10 to 12 minutes or until lightly toasted.

● Transfer to prepared cake pan. Stir in corn syrup and 1 tbsp (15 mL) water until thoroughly coated; stir in apricots and raisins. With spatula, firmly press into even layer. Bake for about 10 minutes or just until dried. Let cool completely on rack. Invert onto back of baking sheet; peel off foil. Invert onto board; cut into bars. Makes 20 bars.

Raspberry Oat Bars

1 cup	all-purpose flour	250 mL
3/4 cup	each quick-cooking rolled oats and packed brown sugar	175 mL
1/4 cup	each wheat germ and natural bran	50 mL
1/2 tsp	each salt and cinnamon	2 mL
1/4 tsp	baking soda	1 mL
1/3 cup	apple juice	75 mL
1/4 cup	vegetable oil	50 mL
3/4 cup	reduced-sugar raspberry jam	175 mL

● In bowl, stir together flour, rolled oats, sugar, wheat germ, bran, salt, cinnamon and baking soda. Drizzle with apple juice and oil; stir until crumbly.

● Press all but 1 cup (250 mL) into greased 9-inch (2.5 L) square cake pan. Spread with jam; sprinkle with remaining oat mixture. Bake in 350°F (180°C) oven for 45 minutes or until golden and jam bubbles at edges. Let cool on rack; cut into bars. Makes 12 bars.

These tasty breakfast or snack bars are less expensive than the foil-wrapped variety found at the store.

Per bar: about
- 195 calories
- 3 g protein
- 5 g fat
- 35 g carbohydrate

Power Bars

2 cups	whole wheat flour	500 mL
1/2 cup	packed brown sugar	125 mL
1/4 cup	skim milk powder	50 mL
1/4 cup	wheat germ	50 mL
1 tsp	baking powder	5 mL
1-1/2 cups	raisins or chopped dried apricots	375 mL
1/2 cup	unsalted sunflower seeds	125 mL
2	eggs	2
1/2 cup	vegetable oil	125 mL
1/2 cup	molasses	125 mL
1/3 cup	peanut butter	75 mL

● In large bowl, stir together flour, sugar, skim milk powder, wheat germ and baking powder; stir in raisins and sunflower seeds. In separate bowl, stir together eggs, oil, molasses and peanut butter; stir into dry ingredients, blending well.

● Spread in greased 9-inch (2.5 L) square cake pan. Bake in 350°F (180°C) oven for 35 minutes or until browned and firm to the touch. Let cool on rack; cut into bars. Makes 24 bars.

There's lots of energy packed into every delicious bite of these satisfying bars.

Per bar: about
- 190 calories
- 4 g protein
- 9 g fat
- 26 g carbohydrate

Caramel Crispy Bars

1/3 cup	unsalted butter	75 mL
1 cup	corn syrup	250 mL
1 tsp	vanilla	5 mL
4 cups	rice crisp cereal	1 L
1 cup	chopped chocolate-coated caramel candy bars	250 mL

● In large saucepan, melt butter over medium heat. Stir in corn syrup and vanilla; cook, stirring, for about 4 minutes or until beginning to thicken. Remove from heat. Stir in cereal and chopped candy.

● Spread in greased 13- x 9-inch (3.5 L) cake pan. Cover and refrigerate for about 1 hour or until firm. Cut into bars. Makes 36 bars.

Chocolate-coated caramel candy bars, stirred right into the crispy batter, make these the best rice cereal squares in town.

Per bar: about
- 80 calories
- 1 g protein
- 3 g fat
- 12 g carbohydrate

Gooey S'mores Squares

22	graham crackers	22
1/4 cup	corn syrup	50 mL
1/4 cup	butter, melted	50 mL
	TOPPING	
3 tbsp	butter	50 mL
4 oz	semisweet chocolate, coarsely chopped	125 g
1	egg	1
1/4 cup	granulated sugar	50 mL
2 tbsp	milk	25 mL
1/2 tsp	vanilla	2 mL
1/4 cup	all-purpose flour	50 mL
1-1/2 cups	miniature marshmallows	375 mL

● Line 8-inch (2 L) square cake pan with foil, leaving 1-inch (2.5 cm) overhang; grease foil. Set aside.

● In food processor, chop crackers into fine crumbs. Add corn syrup and butter; pulse until moistened. Press into prepared pan; bake in 350°F (180°C) oven for 15 minutes or until edges are raised and firm to the touch. Let cool slightly.

● TOPPING: Meanwhile, in bowl over saucepan of hot (not boiling) water, melt butter with 3-1/2 oz (105 g) of the chocolate, stirring occasionally. Let cool to room temperature. With electric mixer, beat in egg, sugar, milk and vanilla; stir in flour.

● Pour topping over base; bake for 20 minutes or until cake tester inserted in center of chocolate layer comes out with moist crumbs. Sprinkle marshmallows evenly over top; broil for 30 seconds or just until lightly toasted. Let cool completely in pan on rack.

● Melt remaining chocolate; dip fork into chocolate, then drizzle over marshmallows. Let stand until set. Using foil as handles, transfer to cutting board. Using knife dipped in hot water and wiped dry, cut into squares. Makes 36 squares.

Crisp Peanut Slices

3 cups	rice crisp cereal	750 mL
1/2 cup	peanuts, coarsely chopped	125 mL
1/2 cup	packed brown sugar	125 mL
1/2 cup	corn syrup	125 mL
1/4 cup	butter	50 mL
2/3 cup	peanut butter	150 mL
1 tsp	vanilla	5 mL
1 cup	semisweet chocolate chips	250 mL
	Chopped peanuts (optional)	

● In large bowl, crush cereal slightly with bottom of cup; stir in peanuts and set aside.

● In saucepan, bring sugar, corn syrup and butter to boil, stirring until smooth; boil for 1 minute, without stirring. Remove from heat.

● Vigorously beat in 1/2 cup (125 mL) of the peanut butter and vanilla until smooth; stir into cereal mixture until combined. Press into greased 8-inch (2 L) square cake pan. Let cool to room temperature.

● In small saucepan, melt chocolate chips with remaining peanut butter; spread over cereal mixture. Sprinkle with peanuts (if using). Refrigerate for 1 hour or until chocolate is set. Cut into bars. Makes 16 bars.

Hazelnut Chocolate Chip Bars ▲

1/2 cup	butter, softened	125 mL
1/2 cup	shortening	125 mL
1 cup	granulated sugar	250 mL
1/2 cup	packed brown sugar	125 mL
2	eggs	2
2 tsp	vanilla	10 mL
2 cups	all-purpose flour	500 mL
1 tsp	baking soda	5 mL
1/2 tsp	salt	2 mL
1-1/2 cups	hazelnuts, toasted and coarsely chopped (see p. 12)	375 mL
1-1/2 cups	jumbo chocolate chips	375 mL

● In large bowl, beat butter with shortening; beat in granulated and brown sugars. Beat in eggs, one at a time; beat in vanilla. In separate bowl, stir together flour, baking soda and salt; stir into butter mixture. Stir in nuts and chocolate chips. Cover and refrigerate for 15 minutes.

● Using fingertips, spread dough evenly into 15- x 10-inch (40 x 25 cm) rimmed baking sheet. Bake in 375°F (190°C) oven for 18 to 20 minutes or until golden brown and still slightly underbaked in center. Let cool slightly on rack; cut into bars while warm. Makes about 50 bars.

For everyone who wants amazing chocolate chip cookies in a hurry, we offer this quickie bar version of a cookie classic.

Per bar: about
- 134 calories
- 9 g fat
- 2 g protein
- 14 g carbohydrate

The Contributors

Photography Credits

LAURA ARSIE: cover photograph of Elizabeth Baird; photograph of the Canadian Living Test Kitchen staff.

FRED BIRD: pages 10, 21, 35, 65, 85, 89.

DOUGLAS BRADSHAW: page 55.

CHRISTOPHER CAMPBELL: pages 40 (top), 42 (how-to photos), 48.

YVONNE DUIVENVOORDEN: page 7.

PAT LACROIX: page 33.

JOY VON TIEDEMANN: page 36.

CURTIS TRENT: page 62.

MICHAEL WARING: page 51.

ROBERT WIGINGTON: front cover; pages 3, 4, 8, 14, 17, 18, 23, 24, 25, 27, 28, 30, 31, 39, 40 (bottom), 41, 42 (cookies), 45, 52, 56, 58, 59, 60, 67, 68, 73, 76, 79, 82.

In the Canadian Living Test Kitchen. Clockwise from left: Elizabeth Baird (food director), Heather Howe (manager), Susan Van Hezewijk, Emily Richards, Donna Bartolini (associate food director), Daphna Rabinovitch (associate food director) and Jennifer MacKenzie.

Special Thanks

Praise and thanks go to the talented and enthusiastic team who put together *Canadian Living's Best Cookies & Squares*. First, to the Canadian Living Test Kitchen staff — home economists Emily Richards, Susan Van Hezewijk, Jennifer MacKenzie and manager Heather Howe — for whom a new cookie, bar or square is always a delicious challenge. Recipe tester Joanne Leese offered a helping hand with the new recipes for this cookbook. Much gratitude is extended to associate food directors Daphna Rabinovitch and Donna Bartolini for their leadership role in testing and creating recipes for *Canadian Living* and for all of the cookbooks.

Appreciation goes also to our valued food writers (noted above), managing editor Susan Antonacci, editorial assistant Olga Goncalves, senior editor Julia Armstrong, our copy department under Michael Killingsworth and our art department guided by Cate Cochran. Special thanks to our meticulous senior food editor, Beverley Renahan, for her high standards of consistency and accuracy and to editor-in-chief Bonnie Cowan and publisher Caren King for their support.

There are others to thank, too. On the visual side — our photographers (noted above); prop stylists Maggi Jones, Janet Walkinshaw, Shelly Tauber, Bridget Sargeant and Susan Doherty-Hannaford, who provide the backgrounds, dishes and embellishments for the luscious food photos; and food stylists Kate Bush, Ruth Gangbar, Debby Charendoff Moses, Lucie Richard, Olga Truchan, Jennifer McLagan, Jill Snider, Sharon Dale and Kathy Robertson, who do the creative baking and garnishing.

Book designers Gord Sibley and Dale Vokey are responsible for the splendid new design of the *Best* Series. Thanks also to Albert Cummings, president of Madison Press Books.

Working with Wanda Nowakowska, associate editorial director at Madison, is always pure pleasure — certainly for her high standard of workmanship and creativity that have made the whole *Best* series so user-friendly and attractive, but also for her calm and always thoughtful, kind and generous nature. Plus, she loves cookies! Thanks also to Tina Gaudino, Donna Chong, Rosemary Hillary and others at Madison Press Books.

Appreciation for their contribution at Random House is extended to Duncan Shields (mass marketing sales manager), Mary Jane Boreham, members of the marketing and publicity departments — Kathleen Bain, Pat Cairns, Sheila Kay, Cathy Paine, Maria Medeiros and Deborah Bjorgan — and to president and publisher David Kent.

Elizabeth Baird

Index

*F*ill up the cookie jar with over 100 of our very best easy-to-make sweet treats

Trust Canadian Living to bring you the **BEST!**